To, Mr. Marian Cierpiala.

From

Salar A. Khan
MD, MBA

Am I Burned Out at Work?

A Self-Care Solution

Salar A. Khan, MD, MBA

Archway Publishing books may be ordered through booksellers or by contacting:

Archway Publishing
1663 Liberty Drive
Bloomington, IN 47403
www.archwaypublishing.com
844-669-3957

ISBN: 978-1-4808-8331-4 (sc)
ISBN: 978-1-4808-8332-1 (hc)
ISBN: 978-1-4808-8330-7 (e)

Library of Congress Control Number: 2019914500

Print information available on the last page.

Archway Publishing rev. date: 10/11/2019

Contents

To my late father, Mukhtar Ahmed Khan.
To my late mother, Noorjehan.
To my children, Faraz Ahmed Khan and Saad Ahmed Khan.
To my wife, Rubina Salar.

Disclaimer

I wrote this book to discuss the workplace burnout that occurs in various professions and provide my insight on this matter through my personal and professional experiences as a physician. Although this book is not meant to be based on research, I hope that you can learn from my experiences in order to deal with any phase of burnout you may be experiencing, or to prevent such occurrences.

Burnout Awareness Song

Who Am I? Why Am I Alive?

Who am I? Why am I alive?
Why do I feel worthless and sad-sad?
Why is my life dull?
Why do I feel empty-empty?
Where has my energy gone?
Why am I sleeping in desperation?
Waking up and thinking twice, calling in sick?
Early retirement sounds great to me.
Who am I? Why am I alive?

Boss is angry, giving me a tough time daily.
Wishing not to face boss.
Daily grind of boring work.
Staying late every day.
Feeling overwhelmed.
Struggling to meet deadlines.
Unable to control my internal conflict.
Who am I? Why am I alive?

My expectation outstrips reality
Like a bad dream.
Unknown fear, shaky confidence.
Unable to finish tasks.

Feeling alone.
A low personal achievement
Causes depersonalization and depression.
Feel like nothing more to give.
Who am I? Why am I alive?

Can anyone tell me what happened to me?
Colleague said I am jaded, frazzled, knackered,
Limp and logy close to burnout.
As I know, no job is ideal.
Now I know I have burned out.

Get back to happy life.
I know why I read the book *Am I Burned Out at Work?*
It is suggested self-care solution to my internal conflict
And assured me it's a treatable condition.
But it needs my full participation.
Never underestimate the power of self-care.
I have control over my health and well-being.
Who am I? Now I know how to defeat my burnout.
Back to a healthy life and enjoying my profession.

A Message from the Author

My goal is to maintain your health and well-being, but it will require your willingness and active participation. To control unrealistic desires and lofty expectations and become burnout-free, follow the self-care solution guidelines in this book.

There is some intentional repetition in prose about the burnout process because most readers do not read a book in one sitting, and they may have underlying burnout. They may lack concentration or focus while reading this book. I tried to make the book simple so nonmedical professionals could benefit from it. In my opinion, repetition of some elements will provide a good continuity to grasp basic concepts related to burnout and make it easy for readers to follow a self-care solution.

Currently, there's no valid, internationally approved definition of burnout. However, burnout has existed at all times and across all cultures. It can happen to anyone anywhere in the world. It is a huge problem in the modern world that is caused when expectations outstrip reality or when work-related conflict erupts between employee and employer. It is a pressing issue in almost all institutions and organizations. Time and money have been spent to find better solutions to prevent burnout, without success. It affects physicians, medical students and residents, nurses, social workers, teachers, lawyers, engineers, caregivers, human resources professionals, police officers, health-care CEOs, and more.

In my opinion, workplace burnout is a dysfunctional or

maladaptive state of mind that presents as a progression that cannot be identified by laboratory tests or diagnostic imaging. No one has yet reached the conclusion that it is purely a medical or psychiatric illness. Workplace burnout is also used interchangeably with life management difficulties, vital exhaustion, overstrain, and workplace exhaustion. The symptoms of vital exhaustion continue daily for two weeks, along with being unable to concentrate, emotional instability, irritability, dizziness, and poor sleep. These factors interfere with a burnout victims' ability to perform jobs. They feel overworked, undervalued, and unappreciated, which gradually erodes their mental capacity and makes them inefficient at work.

Remember that no job is ideal, and workplace burnout is becoming a national epidemic. Our minds and bodies give us warning signs. People experiencing burnout feel overwhelmed, tense, forgetful, frustrated, physically and emotionally exhausted, depersonalized, hopeless, negative, and worthless—all of which lead to severe depression and suicidal thoughts. Burnout is a treatable condition, but it requires the patient's full participation.

Once burnout victims lose the will to survive, negativity will overcome them and control their minds, which will result in decreased self-esteem, motivation, and productivity. This in turn leads to isolation, alcoholism, and drug use, followed by depression and contemplation of suicide when life seems meaningless. Burnout victims are hesitant to seek consultation because these visits may have future adverse effects on their jobs (i.e., mental health stigma). Therefore, some people may be late to seek help or advice and thus may damage their careers by burning out or getting fired from work.

Early onset of burnout can be avoided by maintaining work-life balance, which can be achieved by making changes in daily life event activities. Never underestimate the power of self-care: you have ultimate control over your health and well-being. Severe burnout victims must consult with a psychologist or psychiatrist to receive treatment, which may include antidepressants, psychotherapy, or cognitive behavioral therapy to gain control over severe burnout and to prevent advancement to the suicide phase.

The greatest satisfaction in life often comes from the greatest toil. I have created an identifying formula and self-care solution to cure or control work-related burnout at any organization anywhere in the world. I have also developed a screening tool that primary care physicians can use with their patients to identify early symptoms of burnout in order to manage and prevent its advancement.

Workplace burnout is typically found in human services professions due to their high-stress work environments and the emotional demands of the jobs. High levels of burnout are found among CEOs, the health care sector, social workers, nurses, teachers, lawyers, engineers, customer services representatives, and police officers. Surprisingly, it is associated with highly experienced workers with increased workloads. It appears slowly and is only recognized when it is severe. It appears when workers cannot match the expectations of their jobs, are unable to handle pressure well, and thus experience burnout. Some workers have far greater stressors but effectively deal with them and avoid burnout. In this era, there is too much advancement in economic and industrial growth, fast lifestyles, increased work demand, too many expectations in a short period of time, and incompetent and unprofessional leadership running businesses without respect for human beings and their ability to perform work to match their skills. This leads to psychological stress, which later leads to exhaustion.

Burnout Self-Care Poetry

Stressors are life partners for everyone.
No one lives and survives without stresses.
Life is full of challenges and situational stresses.
Some stresses are blessings to teach you to survive,
And getting a positive outcome,
Leads to motivation and confidence to live—
A key to your success in future.

Don't let stresses go beyond control;
Otherwise, it will be a silent killer,
A culprit of several illnesses that erodes the mind and leads to burnout.
Learn from me the art to cope with stresses and to relax.

Come to me, read this book to navigate your burnout.
Stress reflects through your face, speech, and attitude,
Makes you a negative thinker.
A negative talk of life and compulsively obsessive over details,
Cursing harshness of weather or toughness of life.
Does not know how to nicely deal with truth of life,
Failing to feel sweetness of hardship with success.
A negative attitude creates high stress and low energy,
Makes you irritated and worried.

Unable to finish tasks, high stress pushing into darkness.
Search for strength as a positive thinker,
And learn to move forward.
Honestly analyze weakness and convert it into strength.
Analyze your personality to prevent burnout.
Whether you're extrovert or introvert or in between.
Stress is a culprit of cardiac issues, changing the psychology.
Find your way to relax; everyone has a different nature.

Nature is not the same for all burnout.
Self-cure from burnout is hidden in your personality.
Psychotherapy or psychopharmacology may be supportive.
Learn how to keep happiness inside the heart.
Happiness reflects through your body language,
Your dedication to perform well at work,
Which prevents future burnout.

Learn from the book how to avoid frustration and exhaustion.
Follow my lead to become burnout-free, as an early burnout sufferer.
People knows themselves best,
To find hidden talent and skill sets, to get rid of burnout.

Internal happiness gives relaxation and changing attitude.
Do not be materialistic, which ruins your life.
You are a human, not a robot.
You have feelings and sentiments to reflect expression.
Show the world you are alive, not dead.
Think and find the solution to your burnout.

Have a normal, happy, and healthy life.
Learn to make your career burnout-free.
Find a hidden ability to engage with the world and friends.
Extroverted individuals are less likely to burn out,
Unless having internal conflict causes burnout.

Introverted individuals may have burnout due to isolation—
But isolation provides them space to relax and reduces stress.

Sensitivity to emotion leads to anger, anxiety, and obsession.
Need stability and balance in emotion.
Burnout exhaustion leads to deficient job performance.
Introverts might be overwhelmed but know how to relax.
Boss yells about deficient performance, which is not an attack on character.
Try to do a better job; otherwise, a disturbed behavior leads to isolation,
Indulging in excessive drugs, alcohol, and smoking.
Use your determination to come out of this phase.

Always a solution for all issues, even burnout.
Need to seek correct advice from professionals.
Learn from mistakes; delete fear of failure from mind.
Positive attitude brings back confidence,
Improves job performance and prevents future burnout.

Early burnout starts with a feeling of work overload.
Feeling unvalued person leads to depression,
Leading to spiraling thoughts of suicide,
Giving you bad perception of work environment as your fault,
Failing to prioritize tasks according to merit.
Learn this art to be successful in life.

Read my book—learn a lesson from it.
Make your life easy and perfect
With strong motivation, confidence, and balanced emotions.
To be successful in life and career,
Be assured that you can,
That you can do it effectively and efficiently.

Preface

Recently, I was reading an article related to severe burnout among physicians, medical students and residents, nurses, social workers, teachers, lawyers, engineers, caregivers, human resources professionals, police officers, and health-care chief executive officers (CEOs) who had lost their jobs because they had depression, had contemplated suicide, or had even committed suicide. I felt grief and immediately decided to write this book because these are highly educated professionals who spent their time and money to get to where they are today. To think that after all that, they found their lives to be meaningless came as a shock to me. I realized that this is a pressing issue in almost all organizations and institutions. Burnout is common in any work-related area.

I decided to learn more about this issue. I spoke with top leadership and with intellectuals, and they all said that this is a common workplace issue—and it's only getting worse. I was informed that the workers at their organizations were victims of severe burnout, and these organizations spent much time and money to find better solutions and prevent it.

This encouraged me to look into the topic and review what is known about burnout. I found that several CEOs, medical residents, physicians, and other professionals committed suicide due to severe frustration and depression as a part of this burnout process. I was also surprised to learn that physicians, who are patients' caregivers, are ironically patients themselves. In the midst of their work, they recognize the problem but do not know how to resolve it.

Burnout can result from of a lack of awareness of psychiatric issues, genuine health concerns, and the belief that we should just tough it out. In my opinion, people must have general information about the signs and symptoms related to anxiety and depression so that they can identify early on the psychological change in mind that may be a part of burnout or a disease process.

As a medical student, I remember during my psychiatry rotation that many students were not interested in the subject. This was perhaps because they failed to recognize these symptoms as legitimate health problems. A few years later, as a family practice physician, I noted the significant prevalence of these mental health illnesses. If we had taken these illnesses seriously in medical school, then we would have had a more thorough understanding of common psychiatric illnesses instead of simply referring these patients to psychiatry for further management. Personally, the realness of psychiatric issues and maladaptive states of mind was made apparent. After having worked as a physician, I believe that medical students should take the psychiatric rotation with the mind-set of understanding psychiatric illness in order to treat patients—and so they can become more self-aware of their own states of mind.

After graduating from medical school, it was in my mind to work in various specialties to gain experience and broaden my scope and understanding of rare medical conditions and diseases. In Pakistan, I pursued postgraduate training in internal medicine, neurology, general surgery, and urology surgery. I spent an additional three months in cardiology and dermatology, and I received board certification in pulmonary medicine. I also worked as a psychiatrist at the Karachi Psychiatric Hospital in Pakistan as an attending physician in internal medicine and pulmonology. My role was to differentiate medical illness from psychiatric illness. In this way, I evaluated all mental illness patients to find any underlying medical illness presenting as anxiety or depression. It was a great opportunity to learn and to see diagnosed cases of various mental health conditions. During this time, from December 1985 through December 1987, I diagnosed several pituitary gland adenomas presenting as depression and several thyroid and adrenal gland conditions presenting as anxiety.

In January 1988, when I started a new job under the Ministry of Health in Saudi Arabia as an attending physician in internal medicine and pulmonology, I improved my evaluation of psychiatric and psychological illnesses. I treated many instances of depression and anxiety, ranging from psychotherapy to pharmacotherapy.

I learned to recognize the root cause of these symptoms. I recall a case that may have potentially been a burnout case, but it was not identified as such at the time. I treated this patient from 1983 through 1988 for bronchial asthma. He worked in a bank, and he would always discuss the difficult work environment and constant competition, including his frequent asthma exacerbations. I treated him with anxiolytics and a bronchodilator. His mood and lifestyle improved, however in the end, he retired at the end of 1989.

In my opinion, all physicians should know how to diagnose or screen for mental illness by having a good knowledge of the telltale signs and symptoms of anxiety and mood disorders. This knowledge will also be helpful for physicians themselves if they have early symptoms of burnout. If physicians have this self-awareness, then they can schedule an appointment with a psychologist or psychiatrist. People are hesitant to seek consultations because these visits might have future adverse effects on their jobs (i.e., mental health stigma). This may be why some people are late in seeking advice and thus may damage their careers by becoming burned out or fired from work. At this point, these people must weigh what is important for them: carrying the mental health stigma and ignoring the problem, or identifying and tackling it at its root to improve the quality of their lives. Burnout is being debated in the medical community as to how it should be defined. The tenth revision of the International Classification of Diseases

(ICD-10) lists a separate code for burnout (Z73.0: burnout as a state of vital exhaustion). In ICD-10, burnout has been identified as a factor influencing health status and contact with health services. At the time of this writing, burnout diagnosis was not included in the fifth edition of the *Diagnostic and Statistical Manual of Mental Disorders* (*DSM-V*). Part of the issue is that burnout can look clinically like depression. Although this is true, burnout differs in that its symptomatology is usually secondary to workplace stressors and poor work performance. Here, the difference might be more etiological; in my experience, if it still acts like depression, we should treat it as such. Burnout has a very real effect on people's lives. We should not turn a blind eye to this.

During the last thirty-eight years, I have held various positions as an attending physician, pulmonologist, psychiatrist, chief of medicine, interim director of medical services, interim hospital director, associate professor of medicine, and research compliance director in different organizations from Pakistan to Saudi Arabia to the United States. I have seen and managed many of these cases in my career, and this book will provide you with the tools to recognize and self-manage the symptoms of burnout. Whether you are just starting to feel burned out or have felt this way for years, I hope this book will provide you with some form of a solution. If symptoms significantly worsen, it is important to immediately seek help from a psychiatrist or primary care physician. If the burnout has a strongly suspected component of depression, then there are many good medications available in the market with a doctor's prescription. This will help stabilize your mood and allow you to continue your job efficiently. However, I think it is far more important for you to engage in personal introspection and recognize the root cause of burnout. If that can be identified, you will have taken the necessary first step in resolving it in order to efficiently continue your job. Never underestimate the power of self-management: you have ultimate control over your health and well-being.

Introduction

At any workplace, when employees struggle to meet deadlines, it creates feelings of tension, frustration, hopelessness, negativity, worthlessness, and prolonged stress. It starts with chronic stress until it manifests as burnout. Burnout can lead to depression and then possibly to suicide. Workplace burnout is now becoming a worldwide epidemic that is composed of physical and emotional exhaustion, depersonalization, and low personal achievements.

After reading articles regarding burnout among physicians and general workplace population, I was inspired to write a book to see whether I could determine the mind-set of a burnout victim. Burnout progresses slowly and goes though different phases as it becomes chronic. Prevention should focus on halting the progression and treating the various signs and symptoms of burnout.

The goal is to prevent burnout in potential victims, to self-identify early symptoms and signs related to burnout, and to start self-management according to the level of burnout. If you find yourself close to the onset of burnout, with depression or suicidal thoughts, then immediately seek medical attention. There is a stigma associated with mental health concerns that can stop people from seeking appropriate help. For these people, they need to weigh the possibility of continued suffering versus treatment to get their lives back. It may require some long-term treatment, but the goal is converting your negative cognitive patterns into positive ones with an improved perspective on life.

The scope of this book is to provide everyone suffering from burnout with the guidance and tools to self-manage it.

Burnout is considered a medical diagnosis; however nothing is clear. Symptoms can include the diagnosis of depression, which encompasses extreme fatigue, loss of passion, and intensifying cynicism. This can lead to the inability to manage daily job-related stress. Burnout is a huge problem in the modern world. The World Health Organization identified consistent evidence that high job demands, low control, and effort-reward imbalance are risk factors for mental and physical health problems.[1] Ultimately, burnout results when the balance of deadlines, demands, working hours, and other stressors outstrip rewards, recognition, and the ability to relax.

This book will focus on all aspects of workplace burnout, including the physician's perspective. In my observation and experience, burnout occurs when expectations outstrip reality in the workplace. Every day we all obsess over several expectations that may or may not meet with reality, but it never leads to burnout.

To provide a perspective from my background, medical professionals have many reasons why they may become burned out. US medical education is very costly, and when combined with our dysfunctional health-care system, it leads to many stressors. Younger doctors are straddled with massive debt, which affects how they practice medicine. Senior doctors adjust in varying degrees to the technological changes in medicine. Medicine is supposed to be about healing, but it is run like a business. Many who enter the profession with idealism quickly become jaded. Pharmaceutical companies do business selling lifesaving medications and medical devices to make a profit; in recent memory, the scandal regarding overpricing with the EpiPen demonstrates the misalignment in incentives. Companies frequently cut prices for those in lower socioeconomic brackets, but medications

---

[1] World Health Organization, "Health Impact of Psychosocial Hazards at Work: An Overview," www.who.int/occupational_health/publications/hazardpsychosocial/en (accessed October 24, 2018).

are often still cost prohibitive. At the end of the day, the patient loses, and the physician feels the loss of autonomy and eventual burnout.

I recall numerous times in my professional career when my ideas and plans were met with resistance. I noticed that in the higher rungs of leadership, people are often insecure and will block others from climbing any further, especially in Pakistan. They are concerned about losing their jobs to more enthusiastic and highly motivated employees. This could have caused me to burn out, but I was fine. My goal had always been to do what was best for my patients to the best of my ability.

Robots can replace human beings in the workforce in the near future, especially if we always harp on the lack of resources and bad working environments. These are real concerns, but we must learn how to play with the cards that we have in our hands. Rarely are circumstances perfect, but you must have the confidence to trust your ability to learn and grow. It is also important to see your success stem from your adaptability and gratitude for the opportunity to work and to make a difference, no matter the circumstance. It is a duty, in a way, to push past your limits.

Beyond achieving external success, we must achieve the emotional balance that is key to avoiding burnout. It is the best tool we can use to show compassion and warm feelings toward others and to send a nonverbal message to humanity of how much you care. In my experience, people instinctively try to not show feeling or emotion during high-pressure situations (such as meetings) so that it is not perceived as a weakness. In certain circumstances, such as in politics, this may be an important skill to have. However, constant suppression of emotion can lead to burnout. Always try to balance emotion.

Workplace burnout is influenced by different personalities, thinking styles, attitudes, behaviors, and environments. It can happen to anyone, anytime, and at any workplace. It is a huge problem worldwide when expectations outstrip reality or when there is work-related conflict between employee and employer. My observation and experience taught me that burnout victims are suffering from severe emotional, psychological, and physical exhaustion, with negative attitudes toward work. It begins with acute stress that, if not controlled, converts into chronic stress. It can be best managed by teaching how to change a negative attitude into a positive attitude to neutralize burnout symptoms and to prevent burnout in the long run. You can change the impossible to the possible through intrinsic motivation, confidence in your own abilities, and a strong determination to make changes in your life and work. By reducing high expectations, converting them into reality, and expecting a positive outcome, you will prevent frustration and early burnout. I experienced early burnout symptoms, and I was able to self-manage them. Once burnout victims lose a sense of purpose to survive, then negativity will control the mind, which will reduce self-esteem, decrease motivation, reduce productivity, and start social withdrawal. That in turn leads to isolation, alcoholism, and drug use, followed by depression and contemplated suicide when life seems meaningless. Our minds and bodies give us warning signs. Burnout victims are best able to identify the real cause of chronic stress and deficient performance in the workplace. You can take the first step to resolve burnout at the foundational level by recognizing the signs and symptoms of your burnout. Then, through self-management, you can stop the manifestation of burnout. This book gives you a new angle to control the progression or to even cure the deadly process of burnout so that you can be burnout-free. If burnout is already in an advanced phase, with depression and suicidal thoughts, then immediately contact a psychiatrist because you may need medication to treat this progression of burnout. With your full participation, burnout is mostly a treatable condition.

Burnout is a special type of workplace stress that create doubts about your competence and the value of your work. If you think you might be experiencing workplace burnout, take a closer look at the phenomenon. What you learn through this book might help you face the problem and act before workplace burnout affects your health.

This book provides a quick and easy understanding of the burnout process so that you can make changes in your life and self-manage your burnout. Never underestimate the power of self-management: you have ultimate control over your health and well-being.

Currently, no valid, internationally approved definition of burnout is available, although burnout has existed at all times and across all cultures. It can happen to anyone. It is a subjective complaint of several health issues that lead to decreased accomplishment or performance at work. It is a work-related issue. To date, burnout is not fully considered a psychiatric or medical illness; therefore, it is not mentioned in the *DSM-V*. The ICD-10 code for burnout is listed in the residual category (Z73.0: burnout as a state of vital exhaustion). In 2005, Sweden revised the ICD-10 burnout diagnosis as difficulty in life management characterized by vital exhaustion. The symptoms of vital exhaustion include two weeks of daily experience of decreased energy, difficulty concentrating, irritability, emotional instability, dizziness, and sleep difficulty in addition to these factors interfering with patients' capacity to perform their work responsibilities. In the Netherlands, the term *overstrain* is used to indicate burnout. If the patient has the symptom of exhaustion (lack of energy), then a medical diagnosis of workplace burnout is considered. The Dutch Census Bureau has been assessing burnout among the working class using the index of workplace exhaustion (based on the Maslach Burnout Inventory) in its annual survey since 1997.

The root cause of burnout is embedded into your workplace as a physician, medical student, medical resident, or any kind of worker. If you feel overworked and undervalued, you are at a higher risk of burnout due to erosion of your mental capacity, and you will advance to a true state of burnout.

I hope after reading this book that you will develop a strong personality with a positive attitude and learn how you can fight your stress and frustration to live a normal life with great success at work and with your family. The greatest satisfaction in life often comes from the greatest toil.

Before proceeding with the rest of the book, I highly recommend that you fill out the following self-assessments. These will provide insight into your personality and attitude in addition to determining whether you are experiencing the common signs of burnout. In this way, you can self-evaluate and use this information to guide you as you proceed with the book.

A Self-Assessment to Provide Insight into Your Personality and Attitude

Personality and Attitude Assessment	Yes/No	Comments
Based on my experience and general intuition, I have an ability to judge my boss's attitude and the office environment.		
I have an extroverted attitude when operating in my environment, wanting to know the behavior, actions, and thought processes of the people around me.		
I get positive energy and relaxation from the people with whom I spend time.		
I am introverted and operate internally to process ideas.		
I gain positive energy by working alone and/or operating internally.		
I have a poor work relationship with my boss and coworkers, which leads to negative thinking and emotional imbalance.		
I am intrinsically motivated to try new experiences at work.		
I am happy while I am at work.		

I am reluctant, or lack motivation, to learn new experiences and improve my job skill set.		
I am well organized at work.		
I am dependable at work.		
I am disciplined at work.		
I have a sense of responsibility at work.		
I am target oriented.		
I am willing to accept and own up to my mistakes and learn from them.		
I am easygoing.		
I am kind.		
I am trustworthy.		
I feel close to my coworkers.		
I am not opinionated.		
I am versatile.		
I do not have a cynical attitude toward my boss and coworkers.		
I do not get anxious.		
I feel emotionally stable.		
I do not use alcohol, tobacco, or recreational drugs to relax.		

Scoring: If your answered no to five or more of the questions, then you have qualities that can make you susceptible to burnout.

Burnout Self-Assessment Tool

Burnout Assessment	Strongly Disagree	Disagree	Neutral	Agree	Strongly Agree	Response
I am irritated with my coworkers and/or customers.	1	2	3	4	5	
I am irritated with my boss.	1	2	3	4	5	
I lack the energy to be consistently productive at work.	1	2	3	4	5	
I do not obtain satisfaction from my achievements.	1	2	3	4	5	
I feel disillusioned about my occupation (i.e., my expectation of my occupation did not coincide with the reality of what my work and work environment entailed).	1	2	3	4	5	
I feel that I don't have control at work.	1	2	3	4	5	
My work has unclear job expectations.	1	2	3	4	5	
The workplace dynamics are not conducive to productivity.	1	2	3	4	5	
I feel like my skill set and interests match poorly with my job.	1	2	3	4	5	

Statement	1	2	3	4	5	
My work is very repetitive, dull, or boring.	1	2	3	4	5	
I regularly feel overwhelmed at work.	1	2	3	4	5	
I carry my work-related stress to my home environment (i.e., the stress is reflected in my personality and how I deal with family and friends).	1	2	3	4	5	
I feel isolated at work.	1	2	3	4	5	
Because of work overload and stress, I do not have sufficient time to spend with friends and family.	1	2	3	4	5	
I feel like my work schedule (i.e., eight-hour shifts, night shifts) is interfering with my social life and/or well-being.	1	2	3	4	5	
I am missing my work deadlines because I lack the drive to care anymore.	1	2	3	4	5	
I feel too challenged, or not challenged enough, at work.	1	2	3	4	5	
I have increased irritability and tend to overreact over small mishaps.	1	2	3	4	5	

I do not care about being punctual at work (i.e., arriving to work late and leaving early).	1	2	3	4	5
I wish that I was working somewhere else right now.	1	2	3	4	5

Scoring: < 30 = Not burned out but would welcome a few changes at work; 30–60 = Early phases of burnout; > 60 = Advanced phases of burnout.

Chapter 1

Self-Assessment of Personality

With the proper analysis of personality, along with your unique strengths and weakness, you have a good chance of avoiding burnout at work. As Alison Evans notes in one of her blog entries, "Hone in on your strengths, but don't abandon your weaknesses. Do not neglect one for the other and you will find yourself in [a] strong position to reach your goals at work and in life."[2]

I strongly believe that personality plays an important role in developing future burnout. I do not agree that chronic stress is the key factor of burnout because everyone deals with stress, but not everyone burns out. In this chapter, I will provide background on how you can understand your personality. In this way, we can develop better relationships at work, at home, and with our neighbors, as well as create a more tolerant society. This information will help us understand people at each individual level so that we can learn to respect everyone and avoid injustice.

Personality Types

Personality is the quality of a person or character that often leaves an impression on others. Some personalities are exemplary, and others

---

[2] Alison Evans, "How to Strengthen Your Weakness," Your Employment Solutions, June 24, 2014, https://youremploymentsolutions.com/blog/strengthen-weakness.

are not as much. Each personality has certain attitudes, values, approaches to social relationships, habits, hidden talents, and skill sets in the form of potentials, capabilities, and abilities to perform sophisticated work. In some ways, personality is genetic and can be refined within yourself. Your external and internal environments play the biggest role in defining your personality. You must be honest at the time of self-assessment as you go from challenge to challenge. In this way, you will find hidden abilities that will help you work toward perfection and become a better human being. According to my experience and observation, it will help you refine your self-confidence into an informed intuition. Once you have informed intuition, you become an expert in your chosen profession. In time, you polish your intuition to develop the next level of positive energy. When you engage in positive thinking, you have no fear of failure, and you will communicate confidently and with full command. This leads to clarity of mind and a vision to implement a goal toward a positive outcome. Your passion and intrinsic motivation will be noticed by others and positively influence them.

Psychologists currently use the Big Five model to help explain personality. Ernest Tupes and Raymond Christal first proposed this model in 1961, and its focus is across five domains: openness, conscientiousness, extraversion, agreeableness, and neuroticism.

+ *Openness* is used to mean how likely someone is to engage in imaginative pursuits and to be open-minded. Curiosity is his or her way of life.
+ *Conscientiousness* is used to mean those who are disciplined and have a sense of duty. They are also more organized and prefer to be more decisive versus going with the flow.
+ *Extroversion* is used to mean how sociable and how willing someone is to engage with the world.
+ *Agreeableness* is the capacity to be affable and friendly. Those who represent this trait are easy to get along with. They are less likely to be burned out, however there could be circumstances

in which this is not the case. For example, if someone works in the financial industry (where the focus is on profits), but deep down he or she really wants to work in public health or another area of nonprofit work, then this internal conflict can lead to burnout.

✦ *Neuroticism* describes the tendency of a person to be sensitive to the emotions of anger, anxiety, and obsessiveness. This personality trait has been linked to burnout because these emotions lead to an inability to tackle work challenges. The opposite of this trait is called emotional stability. These people often can have difficult life circumstances and troubled childhoods.

There are a couple of areas I want to discuss from the Big Five model, specifically the role of introversion-extroversion and anxiety in the equation of burnout. First, we will explore the difference between extroverts and introverts.

Extroverts gain energy by engaging with and acting in the objective world. By not engaging with the world and being inactive, their motivation tends to decline. Introverts expend energy by action and gain energy by reflecting. If they spend too much time in action, they will begin to tire.

Introversion and extroversion play a role in burnout. Again, burnout is the loss of productivity in a work environment. An introvert might be more overwhelmed with expectations at work, and so productivity suffers. An extrovert may be able to maintain relations and work but is unable to be productive. This last one might be surprising to consider as a burnout case, and many may suggest it is simply laziness. The heart of burnout comes from losing productivity in the work environment, and being too extroverted can also be a sign that there is another issue. This can be secondary to unresolved personal conflicts. No one is a complete extrovert or a complete introvert, and everyone has elements of both sides in his or her personality. Learning how to balance these two sides is paramount. If people spend too much time in one area, they will begin to feel as if something is missing.

Personalities can also be divided into anxiety and nonanxiety. Some people are more prone to feeling overwhelmed with practical matters. This means that they are more likely to feel as if they are drowning in expectations at work. When a deadline comes, they will feel incompetent. This generates anxiety and a feeling that they lack skill. Being able to identify the triggers for these people is important. They also need to take the time to sufficiently tackle obstacles in bite-size, manageable pieces. These people are also unable to separate the emotional content of the situation from the practical content. For example, when being criticized and yelled at by their boss for not doing their job correctly, anxiety-prone people are more likely to interpret it as an attack on their character instead of viewing it as constructive criticism to do their jobs better in the future.

There are many ways to understand human nature, and personality has had many theories regarding it. One of the most popular is the Myers-Briggs Type Indicator (MBTI), which is based on Jungian typology.[3],[4] There are sixteen personalities according to the MBTI, and they all have a four-letter code (e.g. INTP, ENFJ). The first letter describes where someone is on the introversion-to-extroversion scale, the second letter corresponds to the intuition-to-sensing scale, the third letter to the thinking-to-feeling scale, and the final letter to the judging-to-perceiving scale.

The first letter regarding introversion and extroversion is straightforward. Introverts are most comfortable when they are reflecting on the inner world of ideas and concepts. Extroverts are most comfortable when they are engaging with the world.

The last letter is based on judging and perceiving. *Judging* means

[3] Isabel Briggs Myers and Peter B. Meyers, *Gifts Differing: Understanding Personality Type* (Mountain View, CA: Davies-Black, 1995).
[4] C. G. Jung, *Collected Works of C. G. Jung, Volume 6: Psychological Types* (Princeton, NJ: Princeton University Press, 1971).

that people prefer closure in their affairs and prefer to be decisive. *Perceiving* means that people are more likely to go with the flow.

The middle two letters are based on Jung's description of cognitive functions. According to Jung, human consciousness could be described in terms of four broad categories of cognitive function and is used by people for adaptation and orientation. The four functions are as follows.

1. Sensing (S): Perception by means of immediate apprehension of the objective relationship between subject and object. It is concrete in its workings.
2. Intuition (N): Perception of processes in the background that connect objects—for example, unconscious drives and/or motivations of other people.
3. Thinking (T): Function of intellectual cognition; decision making by forming logical conclusions.
4. Feeling (F): Function of subjective estimation that makes decisions based on value-oriented thinking.

Thus, an ENFJ is someone who is extroverted, intuitive, feeling, and judging. An ISTP is someone who is introverted, sensing, thinking, and perceptive.

The four functions that Jung talks about—the middle two letters in the MBTI—have particular goals. Sensation and intuition help to explain how we understand the world around us, and they are called perceiving functions. The last two functions are how we make decisions and are called judging functions. Each of these four functions also has an extroverted or introverted orientation leading to eight different functions.

1. Extroverted sensing: Focusing on the immediate surroundings and being able to adapt to the situation as it occurs; adaptable.

2. Introverted sensing: Comparing present surroundings to past experiences and in this way building an impressive library of concrete knowledge.
3. Extroverted intuition: Exploring the breadth of possibilities that exist in the objective world. Curiosity and imagination with a focus on integrating with the environment are hallmarks.
4. Introverted intuition: Exploring the connections that exist regarding an object and examining it from multiple angles. A focus on deeply understanding the object.
5. Extroverted thinking: Focusing on being pragmatic, efficient, and goal oriented. The objective is to be integrated into the environment and identifying the rules and principles involved to make decisions. Efficiency is the goal.
6. Introverted thinking: Focusing on understanding the cause and effect behind a system in order to identify rules and principles. In essence, the system must make sense to the person before making a decision. Accuracy is the goal.
7. Extroverted feeling: Making decisions based on building and establishing harmonious relationships. The goal is to build a sense of connectedness, whether with others or more broadly with the world.
8. Introverted feeling: Making decisions based on personal values and trying to ensure that actions and decisions are consistent with one's moral code.

The in-depth explanations of these functions are beyond the scope of this book, however these are the functions that Carl Jung thought were descriptive of patterns of human behavior. Everyone is motivated by very different drivers, and these functions give us a clue as to what those motivations are. Every MBTI personality has four cognitive functions associated with it, and many believe that the first function is what describes the main personality.

For example, people INTJ, their first function is introverted intuition, which means they define themselves as wanting to understand the importance of the purpose and meaning behind things. If people are ESTJ, then their first function is extroverted thinking, and their focus is on being efficient and productive.

The other three cognitive functions can be thought of as helpers that allow the first function to accomplish its goal. In theory (although there is debate regarding this), each of these functions in the personality can be developed. If they are not developed, then burnout results.

For example, it is thought that the first function is always in tension with the last function. An ESTP MBTI personality type function stack leads with extroverted sensing, so the last function is introverted intuition. Extroverted sensing focuses on experiencing and adapting to the world around you. However, the last function provides tension in the personality, so an ESTP will at some point feel a pull to have a greater purpose in one's life rather than simply experience the immediate reality. This tension could lead to indulging in alcohol or drugs to run away from problems at work or at home. This destructive behavior can be evidence of burnout. These people are also more prone to being too extroverted and may frequently switch their jobs.

The solution is often to work on these functions in order, from the first function to the last function. In theory, these functions help to cover the others' blind spots. In an ESTP case, people would work on their second and third functions, introverted thinking and extraverted feeling, respectively.

In the Myers-Briggs system, there are sixteen personalities, and each has four cognitive functions, as noted earlier. In theory, they all have a particular role in how the personality manifests. However, there is much controversy over how these functions manifest or whether they are real at all. Still, many people have been able to use these dynamics to understand themselves.

The Significance of Knowing Your Strengths and Weaknesses

Part of personality is knowing your strengths and weaknesses. Often a strength can be a weakness, and a weakness can be a strength.

In burnout, there is often a mismatch between work and your strengths and weaknesses. Personal character also plays a role. Depending on how refined you are, you can be strong and confident or weak and shaky. Knowing your personality helps you to make good decisions due to the ability to focus completely as well as greater self-awareness.

Strengths are a tool to select your field of interest to become successful. For example, if you are good in calculations and mathematics, then engineering or banking could be a good fit. If your interest is in helping the community and easing the suffering of people, then nonprofit work or the medical field could be your choice. Being clear about your strengths helps you see yourself realistically and accomplish your goals by being more positive and confident.

Thus, the job and your strengths must match. Sometimes we lie or convince ourselves we want a job because of the status and not necessarily because we care about the work. If you cheat yourself in this way while applying for the job, then you will certainly run into trouble. This leads to a higher risk of burnout. Please be honest. It is also necessary to evaluate how the company and its mission will benefit from your strengths. Think about your organizational skills, collaborative skills, time management skills, self-confidence, and accountability to yourself.

I believe that the following qualities are important strengths to be successful in a career: no fear of failure, highly organized, disciplined, self-confident, strong faith in abilities, goal and target achiever, clarity of vision, hyperfocused, strategic thinker, intrinsically motivated, open-minded, ability to inspire people, strong determination, quick learner, and compassion.

These strengths will develop over time. There will be many weaknesses to tackle, but learning to control those weaknesses is important.

This is because they then become strengths and lead to improvement in decision-making and efficiency. As I see my accomplishment, it becomes my strength. Nothing is impossible and everything is possible. That is the greatness of human beings.

I have several weaknesses, but I have more strengths. Sometimes I lose patience, don't tolerate criticism, and take things personally. However, I know I can manage these situations and learn from them. This also means that I gain some level of control over them. With experience and exposure to various scenarios, the mind learns to analyze its mistakes and to evolve. In this way, fear of failure disappears.

Your strengths and weaknesses are always fluctuating, depending on the situation and environment. At the time of decision making, your intuition and background information will hone your instinct to make the correct decision. It is a daily process to work on and improve your strengths and weaknesses.

Chapter 2

Burnout Etiology and Research

Workplace burnout results from unresolved, continuous emotional and interpersonal chronic stress. You must be able to view this stress through various new angles to gain a deeper understanding of workplace burnout. This is accompanied by feelings of exhaustion, cynicism, and inefficiency. Burnout is common among professional groups of people, including physicians, medical students and residents, nurses, social workers, human resources professionals, CEOs, teachers, lawyers, engineers, customer service representatives, and police officers. Other groups of people also experience burnout, such as parents, spouses, and caregivers. Burnout can damage your work environment as well as your home and social life.

In 1974, Herbert Freudenberger was the first researcher to use the term *burnout* in a psychology-related journal.[5] His paper was based on his observations of the volunteer staff, including himself, at a free drug addicts clinic. He characterized burnout symptoms as exhaustion due to too many work demands as well as physical symptoms like headaches, poor sleep, and quickness to anger. He observed that the burned-out worker looks, acts, and seems depressed. After publication of this paper, interest grew in occupational burnout. The term was also used in the title of a 1961 Graham Greene novel, *A Burnt-Out*

---

[5] Herbert J. Freudenberger, "Staff Burn-Out," *Journal of Social Issues* 30, no. 1 (1974): 159–65, doi:10.1111/j.1540-4560.1974.tb00706.x.

Case, which dealt with a doctor working in the Belgian Congo with patients who had leprosy.[6] Later, Maslach and her colleagues focused on burnout within human service professions (e.g., teachers, social workers).[7] She later expanded the application of burnout to include workers in many other occupations.

The Maslach Burnout Inventory (MBI) was published in 1981. This valuable tool is used to determine the various phases of burnout and is an industry-leading assessment and research instrument. This MBI helps to measure employee well-being at work. This assessment can be completed in fifteen minutes. The inventory has three sections, with twenty-two items that represent personal feelings or attitudes. There is a separate scoring system. If you feel stress, fatigue, and irritability, the MBI can be taken to assess your well-being.

+ **Section 1:** Emotional exhaustion is affecting your mental and physical health due to various internal and external factors. The clinical presentation of emotional exhaustion is being unable to make decisions, having impaired judgment, and self-forgetfulness. This section of the MBI has nine items.

+ **Section 2:** Depersonalization: Burnout victims become detached and empathetic with other employees. It is also known as compassion fatigue. The clinical presentation of depersonalization is anger, negativity, and increased irritability. This section of the MBI has five items.

+ **Section 3:** Reduced personal accomplishment due to feelings of inefficacy and loss of purpose. The clinical presentation of burnout victims is reduced self-esteem, which leads to decreased motivation, decreased productivity, and withdrawal. This section of the MBI has eight items.

---

[6] Graham Greene, *A Burnt-Out Case* (New York: Penguin, 1960).

[7] Christina Maslach and Susan E. Jackson, "The Measurement of Experienced Burnout," *Journal of Organizational Behavior* 2, no. 2 (1981): 99–113, doi:10.1002/job.4030020205.

Maslach and her collaborators developed six components that contribute to burnout in the workplace environment: workload, control, reward, community, fairness, and values. If one or more of these components is chronically mismatched between employee and employer, it erodes one's passion. There is a direct link between high job demands and fewer job resources; thus, the employee feels a loss of control and fails to achieve tasks on time.

Burnout is often work specific, but it can be found in students as well. Burnout appears to be caused by excessive long-term psychological or physical stress and emotional arousal. It is most common in service professions, such as nursing and teaching, and in jobs that involve a lot of customer relationships where emotions are suppressed. The depersonalization aspect of burnout may be a mechanism designed to protect against the effects of excessive emotional arousal. This is achieved by treating the other party as an object rather than as a person. Different personalities, thinking styles, attitudes, behaviors, and home environments influence burnout.

The following analogy will help to simplify the mechanisms of burnout. Let's say you are preparing for work in the morning, and you put bread slices in a toaster. Then you set the proper heat according to how well toasted you want your bread: light brown, moderate brown, or dark brown. This example will help you to understand the process of burnout. In the early phases in the toaster, the bread turns from light brown to moderate brown. However, your mind slips, and you don't realize the bread is burning until it is too late. It comes out black, and you grudgingly eat it. The early phase of light-brown bread is the phase in which everyone in the organization likes you, and you are motivated to continue working and pushing yourself. Soon, however, the workload continues to pile up, and you begin to feel tension and pressure. Now simple stress turns into chronic stress, frustration, and exhaustion, and you are like burned bread. Similarly, your boss may not fire you because you are still productive, but once you are completely burned out, draining employee morale and ruining the company reputation, you will be fired. Like burned bread, our inclination is to toss it out; everyone's opinion at the workplace is similar, and you are now a drag on resources. You are irritable, frustrated, and unable to work within a team. Now that you feel your value is worse than burned bread, you will feel hopeless and start to contemplate suicide.

Burned toast is no way to enjoy your breakfast. You naturally want to toast bread optimally. You have feelings and desires that exist inside your heart. When you first begin a job, you come with a hope to see your future career in this organization. At this point, you have a desire to be integrated with your colleagues and to be helpful toward everyone. But later, once things are not under your control or you feel your expectations are gone, work becomes a chore. You begin to hate your job, losing interest in it and developing an irritable attitude. During this entire phase, the feelings of the heart merge with the mind. In the beginning, there was positive synchrony between the two, leading to high-octane energy in your body. This leads to a shift in perspective, and the world looks beautiful: you have ideas about vacation, enjoying natural beauty, or going on long drives.

Once you notice your expectations are not met, then the positive feelings fade and convert into negative feelings. As you see the world through dark glasses, you lose hope and move toward depression.

If you have an anxious personality and your work environment is unfavorable, then this will add additional stress at work. Now you have developed apprehension in your work environment, which will make you burn out sooner. Other particular stresses that can lead to burnout are feelings of being permanently overworked (subjectively or objectively), limited challenges at work, pressure to perform, conflict with coworkers, and overcommitments that cause you to neglect your own needs.

When Expectations Do Not Meet Reality

An expectation is a firm belief that a potential future outcome will be a part of our reality or that of others. Our lives begin with expectations. We place expectations on ourselves and on others in order to succeed in reality. For instance, you may expect your spouse to prepare breakfast every morning before you wake up. The day that your spouse fails to do so, you may become irritated because of your ingrained expectation. With careers, you may envision your success at a new job and an opportunity to build your career.

Expectation is an anxiety-generating state because we consider driving a favorable outcome, which could be our hopes, dreams, or beliefs for the future, whereas reality is the actual outcome. In my observation, there is a middle phase between expectation and reality, which is a feeling of stress or anxiety. If you are working on a huge project that needs months or years to be completed, and you are directly involved in that project as a key player, then you are generating several fears about outcome. Negative thoughts will shake your confidence and blur your clarity of mind. Naturally, you will cultivate stress with fear, and if it continues long enough, it becomes chronic stress, which leads to the onset of burnout. If the reality of this expectation becomes disastrous, then you will feel that your energy is drained and that your false expectations appear as real in your life. Once you have developed fear and stress, you must begin to reassure yourself with positive thinking that everything will be fine and that you are working hard to convert expectations into reality, with determination and faith in your abilities. Think about other positive outcomes of life that you converted into reality to encourage yourself and to generate positive feedback in your mind. In this way, you can get whatever you want to get. It is simply a matter of continuing your self-motivation with self-confidence. In the beginning, when you set goals for your expectations, you have designed an achievable goal with a realistic approach that will prevent burnout.

At the beginning of my career, my expectations did not meet

reality many times. I was under tremendous stress and lost confidence in my own abilities. I immediately decided to analyze my weaknesses in order to convert my expectations into reality. I found many loopholes in my plan, and I decided to correct them all and then start again with strong determination. This time I was able to convert my expectations into reality, which boosted my confidence and added to my skill set. I was ready for the next challenge.

As shown in Figure 1, there is always a period of stress or anxiety between expectations and reality. We can overcome our stress while working on a huge project by clearly focusing on daily tasks and their completion in order to move toward achieving reality as a positive outcome.

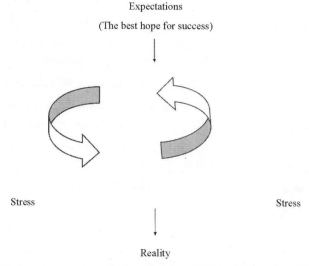

Figure 1. Reality may be disastrous and lead to negative thinking, loss of self-confidence, and reduced self-motivation, precipitating the process of early burnout.

I gave a task to my team at work to complete a project by a certain date and time. Usually they achieve tasks on time, but this time they didn't. This meant that this time, my expectations were not fulfilled. I was upset about it. I analyzed myself to see whether it was my fault—whether I had poorly communicated the instructions to the team—so that next time my expectations would create a positive reality. In my opinion, expectations are bilateral. An organization expects us to meet its vision and mission for profit or other goals, but we also have expectations of it meeting our career goals and well-being.

The other half of the coin is reality. Reality is any outcome that has come into existence. If it appears as a failure, it will add to your stress and shake your confidence, but if it is a positive outcome, then you will find hidden talents and new skill sets within yourself, which will further improve your vision and clarity of mind. This leads to additional gains in self-confidence, resulting in more positive results and ultimately in internal happiness. The future cannot be known until we put in the work and see how it manifests in reality. We can simply hope for the best and do extraordinary work to convert dreams into reality.

I worked alone on several occasions when other staff members were not willing to participate in a project because there was no extrinsic reward attached to it. My supervisor looked to me. I undertook the challenge to find my hidden abilities to fulfill the workplace expectations and convert reality into a strong positive outcome. It was a huge accreditation project for a research program to meet 102 standards and 257 elements. From the beginning, I set my expectations to receive a score of 100 percent. I worked six extra hours daily for four months to prepare the department for this task. During this period, I did my daily job duties as well. I tried hard to meet all requirements with a high efficiency rate while clarifying in my mind how to get excellent results. I faced a lot of troubleshooting with a lot of stress and anxiety, but I managed with intrinsic motivation and self-confidence, which I used as a CEO in Saudi Arabia. My mind was training due to handling a diverse situation with enormous success. In the end, the final outcome of this expectation was receiving a score of 100 percent, making my dream come true and proving that expectations can meet reality. This boosted my self-confidence, enhanced my motivation, and readied me to accept additional challenges. Our research program was the only one that got a 100 percent score nationwide. It was possible only because of a strong commitment and dedication to the work, but there was an equal chance that it could have failed, with a disastrous reality resulting. I had strong faith on my abilities, and I had the motivation and desire to sacrifice six hours every day for four months.

All projects start with an expectation in any organization, and the team works hard to shape this expectation into reality. This leads to accomplishment and success. Each success boosts our morale and confidence and prepares us to accept another challenge (expectation) to convert into reality.

To make clear my concept about expectations, let's divide it into two components.

+ *Failure of expectations*: The anticipation of an event that we do not want to accept because of our behavior, and that makes success a difficult destination to reach. We never accept failure as a learning tool to further improve and progress toward a reality that we can call an enormous success. If we were not successful, then our negative results or failures become a stepping stone to our future successes through an honest analysis of our mistakes.

+ *Successful expectations*: We are ambitious and have many dreams regarding our careers to accomplish our goals. We must be equally intuitive and internally motivated to meet reality. In this pathway, we have to be prepared for dealing with various upsets and stresses, and we must remain hyperfocused on our expectations.

At the start of a job, we are primed to change the world, even though we are simply beginners at this stage. You have to learn with passion what your work duties are, focus on improvement, be eager to learn new things on a daily basis, and seek clarification when needed so that you can gain control over your work. Do not expect to attain a higher position overnight. Try to do your job with a positive attitude. The first job is hard, so gain valuable learning experience. Remember that no job is perfect. If people are paying you for your job, then they have an expectation of superior performance. In the corporate world, expectations can be high in the work environment, so performance is paramount. Remember, expectations may not always meet reality. It depends on several factors, including employing thinking and organization (employer) thinking.

With employee thinking, not all jobs give you what you want or expect. The hours worked, the quality of the work environment, and the stress level are directly related to workload. Think about your goals. Everyone is looking for job security and a stable job. Soon you realize that you know nothing and that a college education has no value in achieving a positive outcome at work. If you are not eager to learn, then you have no idea what needs to be done. People work hard because they want to earn a living.

With organization (employer) thinking, good employers always value their employees. They strive to provide the resources necessary to accomplish daily tasks. They appreciate their employees and monitor and recognize their efforts so that employees can perform well. Some employers do not care about your degree of improvement and level of confidence as they pertain to your career development. They provide you with improvement in your organizational skills and build confidence for your future career. Your college education prepared you to some extent to tackle challenges in your future occupations. The organization's expectations of you are to meet the work requirements on a daily basis. In the beginning, you are extremely motivated, and you love the company and the boss. However, your supervisor is constantly watching to see whether you make any mistakes, and you have to provide justification for any mistakes. You are under pressure and afraid of making another mistake because you will be reprimanded.

Always be prepared to immediately resolve any issue at your workplace from the very beginning by using excellent interpersonal communication. Communication allows you to stay alert to any negative feedback so that you can correct it right away before things get worse. If you got poor work remarks or feel work overload and have obsessive compulsiveness, and by virtue of this you cannot find ways to improve yourself, then consulting the supervisor is the best way to resolve performance issues. If you are not good in one job, it is likely that you cannot manage another new job. If you feel that you hate your job and that long working hours and the workload makes you unhappy, then you need to analyze yourself to correct it, or seek advice from a psychologist, prior to getting another job.

We all have various kinds of expectations of one another. Expectations are a strong belief in attaining future positive results. An example is students who have high expectations of their future careers. Another example is customer satisfaction that reflects the expectations and experiences the customer has with a product or service. Expectations reflect both past and current product evaluation by the customer. This depends on how the product was marketed. To create a marketing strategy, information must be gathered from multiple sources so that the company can present the product in the best light and meet consumers' expectations. Parents expect their kids to keep up their grades in school. Educational institutions try to keep high standards of education so that they can maintain their high ranks nationwide, financial institutions have expectations to maximize profits, and businesses are always trying to expand their scope and earn more. Quite a few organizations earn a high level of success as a reality. As stated earlier, the burnout process begins because expectations outstrip reality.

I have noticed that various categories of expectations are utilized in evaluating products' predictability in the market after customer experience surveys are used to determine the future expectations of those products to achieve reality. Understanding the following seven customer expectations is critical before you set out to measure customer satisfaction.[8] In my personal experience and observation, these seven categories are also highly relevant to burnout victims. Exploring them will help to better understand the process of burnout.

Categories of Expectations in Relation to Burnout Victims

The following discussion includes various business model categories of expectation, which fit with the beginning of the burnout process.

Category 1: Explicit Expectation

This is defined as a very clear detail without any flaws or doubts. Most successful organizations and institutions have clear vision and mission statements that are to be met by all employees. They have well-defined performance standards. These are fast-paced workplace environments. The organization's expectation is for each employee to meet the needs of the organization. If there is a mismatch between employees' experience and skill sets, or if employees fail to meet daily deadlines to accomplish their work, it will produce an extra burden, and employees will gradually feel pressure and tension. If employees are unable to cope with this situation, then it will lead to burnout. The best example of providing explicit expectations of all employees, supervisors, and CEOs are the health-care organizations, financial institutions, and academic institutions. Employees of these organizations all must meet high standards, which may cause tension, pressure, stress, feelings of being overwhelmed, and exhaustion, which may be felt continuously for eighteen to twenty-four months. It causes

---

[8] Scott Smith, "Customer Expectations: 7 Types All Exceptional Researchers Must Understand," Qualtrics, March 2, 2018, www.qualtrics.com/blog/customer-expectations.

chronic stress when employees are unable to manage tension in the early phase and then proceed to severe burnout.

Category 2: Implicit (Silent) Expectation

This is defined when expectations are not stated but are a silent understanding. Implicit expectations reflect established norms of performance. Implicit expectations are established by business in general, other companies, industries, and even cultures. An implicit reference might include such wording as "Compared with other companies ..." or "Compared to the leading brand ..." In this situation, employees must keep up the work pace to meet the organization's silent expectations. If some employees are unable meet these expectations, then they will be held accountable and become stressed. This failure to cope will lead to the early onset of burnout. Financial institutions are the best example of this category.

Category 3: Static Performance Expectations

Static performance expectations address how performance and quality are defined for a specific application. Performance measures related to quality of outcomes may include the evaluation of accessibility, customization, dependability, timeliness, accuracy, and user-friendly interfaces. If employees are unable to meet this type of expectation because they are not challenged and not motivated to perform well, then being held accountable by the employer can lead to stress and begin the process of early burnout.

Category 4: Dynamic Performance Expectations

This is defined as how the product or service is expected to evolve over time. Dynamic expectations may be about changes in the support, product, or service needed to meet future business or use environments. It may help to produce static performance expectations as new uses, integrations, or system requirements develop and become more stable. Some organizations are vibrant and maintain a fast pace to meet market needs. To survive in a competitive market, their employees must work in a demanding environment to meet the daily needs of the organization. If employees are unable to meet this demand, then stress will start and lead to the onset of the burnout process.

Category 5: Technological Expectations

An example here is on using and becoming familiar with modern health-care technology, such as patients' electronic medical records (EMRs) or mobile phones. This technology is continually evolving, leading to higher expectations of new features. The older generation of doctors has difficulty managing EMRs and finds them time consuming. This quickly becomes frustrating, which leads to burnout. They do not have time to pay more attention to patients and their care. It is also reported that older generations of physicians who are less familiar with this electronic interface easily go into burnout, which can lead to early retirement.

Category 6: Interpersonal Expectations

Working in a big organization and dealing with various institutions, as well as interorganizational departments, leads to the necessity of good interpersonal relationships in order to accomplish the organization's goal. It also reflects the relationship between the customer and the product or service provider as a health-care organization for patients. Person-to-person relationships are increasingly important, especially where products require support for proper use and functioning.

Support expectations are also mandatory to prevent employee burnout, including interpersonal sharing of technical knowledge, ability to solve a problem, ability to communicate, reduced time to problem resolution, courtesy, patience, enthusiasm, helpfulness, assurance that they understood the problem and the situation, communication skills, and customer perceptions regarding professionalism of conduct, often including image and appearance.

Category 7: Situational Expectations

In building a customer satisfaction survey, it is also helpful to evaluate why prepurchase expectations or postpurchase satisfaction may or may not be fulfilled or even measurable. The downsizing of an organization can lead to situational stresses. Perhaps the division you are working for had half of its workforce cut, and you are worried that you might be next. It is also possible that you might have more work assigned to you, especially if divisions are being merged or the company is planning to move in a different direction.

Professions Prone to Burnout

Those employed at any workplace, from the lowest skilled worker to the most highly skilled (such as a CEO, supervisor, and manager), can experience burnout. Occupational burnout typically occurs in human services professions because of high-stress work environments and the emotional demands brought about by working with others. Surprisingly, occupational burnout is associated with highly experienced workers with increased workload. It appears slowly, recognizable only when it is severe. It appears when workers cannot match the expectations of a job with few stressors, they are unable to handle pressure well and experience burnout—whereas another worker has far greater stressors but effectively deals with them and avoids burnout.

In this era, there is too much advancement in economic and industrial growth, a fast-paced lifestyle, an increase in work demands, and great expectations in a brief period. With incompetent, unprofessional leadership running businesses, and doing so without common human respect or the ability to match employee skills with the ability to perform the work, this leads to psychological stress among employees, which later develops into exhaustion. Currently, economic values are greater than human values. Some may decry this, however this is reality.

In my personal experience and observation, the most common factor that leads to burnout is a mismatch between job functions and the employee. Doing too much with few resources and going beyond personal limits may be due to a company's desire to downsize. It all comes down to job demands and job resources. Job demands are the physical and psychological costs of work, such as work pressure and emotional demands. This leads to disengagement at work. Burnout is found in all kinds of jobs.

I have created an identifying formula and self-management guidelines to cure or control work-related burnout at any organization anywhere in the world. This is a psychological condition that affects educated and professional groups of people, and it must be treated based on psychoanalysis of each individual personality to find the cause(s) behind the onset of burnout and to customize a self-management plan by intercepting each stage of burnout to cure or at least control its progression. If it is complicated by mental illness, then it must be treated with medication prescribed by a psychiatrist. This is a problem that has far-reaching consequences; resources have been spent to prevent the issue but with little success. It is a leading cause of the increased number of suicides, resulting in the loss of highly educated and professionally talented human beings. This is more common than we assume with physicians and medical residents. In the beginning of their careers, they are highly enthusiastic, determined to make a difference in the health-care system, displaying positive energy that leads them to take on more and more work, working extra hours to accomplish assignments, and sometimes surpassing the output of two to three people to show that they are highly competent. During this period, the organization's leadership never appreciates these employees; they are considering the big picture and trying to optimize the product or service, which at times leads to automation and a shrinking number of human beings who do the work. Or if a company is not making enough profit, it starts downsizing and reducing resources to cut costs. As this occurs, employees become more dispirited because at some level, there was an expectation of getting extra money, external awards, and promotions. Losing those expectations stamps out their desires and wishes to progress in a career. Now the negative feelings start, such as wondering why they should do extra work and spend extra time with no appreciation. This is the beginning of burnout: all positive thinking has been converted into negative thinking, and employees are less productive at work. Internally, rejection and frustration start.

Prior to this incident, employees were attaining excellent job performance and taking on additional projects with the expectation of extra salary. If this extra compensation isn't received, they start feeling stressed, overwhelmed, and frustrated. If it continues, it will lead to more negative feelings that will eventually result in depersonalization, cynicism, detachment, isolation, and alcohol and drug use. This is followed by depression and, in extreme cases, suicide.

Workplace burnout is thought to result from long-term, unresolved job stress. Numerous factors are responsible for burnout, including emotional exhaustion, physical fatigue, depersonalization, or disengagement.

Burnout is mental, emotional, and physical exhaustion due to working a fast-paced, demanding job for an extended period, which leads to chronic stress. Burnout makes it difficult to function effectively on both personal and professional levels. Burnout can occur slowly and so can be sometimes hard to recognize, although our minds and bodies give us warning signs. Biologically, we know that stress hormones increase in burnout. In particular with stress, cortisol is released into our bloodstream.

There are two types of stresses.

Eustress

Burnout results from stress, but defining that stress becomes tricky. Some people work great under stress, with increased productivity. Therefore, I use the term *stress reaction* as the ability to accomplish a task and to motivate oneself to perform well. Stress is a part of our daily life, and if we embrace this stress in a positive way, it is known as eustress. Eustress is when I prepare at work for my targets for the day. As I accomplish them, I gain energy and excitement as I work to accomplish my targets one after another. In this way, I keep rolling with positive energy. This stress gives me pleasure. The challenge isn't restricted to only my job; it also encompasses working with others in a socially graceful way.

Stress is the basis for how most people respond to danger, which prepares them to face a threat or to flee to a safe environment. It will give you self-confidence to protect the future when there is a higher threat level.

Pathological (Negative) Stress

Some people fail to manage the initial onset of stress. They never come out from it, which causes chemical changes in the body, including high blood pressure, palpitations or increased heart rate, and even increased blood sugar. Everyone experiences stress from time to time as a result of emotional, mental, and physical pressures. However, when these factors become continuous, this translates into chronic stress, which can damage your health and cause headaches, sleeplessness, sadness, anger, irritability, and gastric upsets. Later, it advances to burnout.

If you are unable to achieve your expectations at work, your mind will start processing negativity toward work. Now you will become a negative thinker and be unable to control stress, which will lead to chronic stress and frustration. Stress may be internal due to individual personality, such as overly health-conscious people, obsessive personality, hysterical personality, psychosomatic illness, and hypo-chondriasis. I treated thousands of medical illness and psychiatric patients, but I never met a patient with these illnesses who presented as a burnout patient. Although they have chronic illness with chronic stress, they do not have frustration or depersonalization of self as seen in burnout victims. Chronic illness contributes to negative think-ing, including that patients may not be cured of an illness, a fear of death, or suicidal thoughts due to an illness that is not responding to treatment.

This can be due to lack of appreciation and self-reflection on having a poor skill set. Label your emotions. This is important so that you can find solutions for managing them. Reach out for help as needed and be motivated to learn. Consider switching jobs if the work mismatch is too much.

I managed several patients with chronic stress who were suffering from end-stage cancer, hypertension, diabetes mellitus, and other chronic conditions, but they did not present as suffering from burn-out. For me, it means there is something else going on in the mind of the person who will be a future burnout victim.

Any organization that hires employees for a higher-level position, such as manager, supervisor, CEO, and physician, has an expectation from its employees to meet the organization's vision and mission. Once new employees achieve these goals for the organization, trust in and respect for the organization will develop within the employee. This is the best tool to predict future success in an organization.

Unless you work for a very maligned organization, if the situation was the opposite and the employee was not meeting the organization's goals, then the organization will not listen to any reason (even if gen-uine) for betterment. You will become discouraged, and that erosion of individual personality leads to future burnout.

If the employee is self-confident and self-motivated, then one can expect success. This employee will develop an attitude of positive thinking in the workplace, along with specific coinciding behavior. If work expectations are not met, then it will cause anger, disgust, and dissatisfaction among colleagues.

Communicate expectations through voice and body language. Expectations affect people's perceptions. Expectations are assumptions that require confidence in your abilities. Use your past experiences and accomplishments to reassure yourself of your abilities.

The meaningful ideas of expectation, persuasion, and reinforcement are the foundation for building confidence in employees if the immediate boss is giving honest feedback, such as "You can do it," "You're doing great," and "I'm happy with your progress." This will develop internal motivation to accomplish tasks within the timeline, leading to the foundation of your career. If you are doing an extraordinary job, then the boss appreciates your work performance. It will provide you with confidence to take on a more challenging job. Praise is an effective psychological tool that leaders can use to encourage self-motivation in employees who are about to burn out. If the boss is not forthcoming, then you can analyze yourself to see how you can meet the organization's expectations or move on from the job position.

In my experience, perception is the state of being or the process through which we become aware of the intuition needed to interpret external stimuli through neurophysiological processes, including memory. Researchers would like to look into other aspects of the lives of those who have developed burnout. There may be some influence related to cultural background, family style, and personality. For example, people with suspicious personalities may have gotten the wrong perception from a supervisor that they are being assigned more work without any appreciation or awards. This will manifest with tension, pressure, and overwhelming feelings, and negative thinking about the supervisor will begin. At this phase, the early burnout process will start due to this perception, although the reality may be different.

A Conceptual Model of Burnout

The following conceptual model will help you understand where psychiatrists and medical researchers are in terms of the almost epidemic situation of workplace burnout.[9] The burnout process goes through three dimensional models.

+ The first dimension of burnout is exhaustion, which stems from increase demand and workload.
+ The second dimension of burnout is detachment or depersonalization or cynicism, which stems from a negative reaction to people and to the job.
+ The third dimension of burnout is inefficiency, which stems from feelings of inadequacy and failure and leads to reduced personal accomplishment or professional inefficacy.

This model is based on work stress due to an imbalance between job and life. The imbalance appears between work demands and individual sources or strain as an emotional response to exhaustion and anxiety. You have a deficiency in coping, which leads to behavior and attitude changes and to an advancement in cynicism. There is another important factor leading to burnout based on resource imbalance. The researchers clearly identified six areas of workplace imbalance that must be addressed by the employer to prevent burnout: workload, control, reward, community, fairness, and value. Any mismatch in these areas leads to less effective job performance and a change in social behavior and in personal well-being.

If these employers properly address these six areas from the start, I am sure we can eliminate workplace burnout in the future. We need sincerity and honesty from both parties, the employer and the employee, to ensure the prevention of burnout. We also need help

---

[9] Christina Maslach and Michael P. Leiter, "Understanding the Burnout Experience: Recent Research and Its Implications for Psychiatry," *World Psychiatry* 15, no. 2 (2016): 103–111.

from psychologists and psychiatrists to establish whether burnout has a mental illness component or whether the clinician will allow a medical diagnosis of burnout without the mental health stigma.

The researchers used the diagnosis of vital exhaustion to receive reimbursement through insurance for treating patients suffering from burnout. In northern Europe, such as Sweden and the Netherlands, the clinical diagnosis of neurasthenia or chronic fatigue is used for burnout. Sweden has been using the term *workplace neurasthenia* for burnout since 1997. North America is reluctant to recognize burnout as a clinical diagnosis because of disability coverage.

Chapter 3

Workplace Burnout

In this chapter, I will focus on the mind-set of a burnout victim towards workplace stress and poor work performance.

Workplace burnout is typically found in human services professions due to their high-stress work environments and the emotional demands of the jobs. High levels of burnout are found among CEOs, the health care sector, social workers, nurses, teachers, lawyers, engineers, customer services representatives, and police officers. Surprisingly, it is associated with highly experienced workers with increased workloads. It appears slowly and is only recognized when it is severe. It appears when workers cannot match the expectations of their jobs, are unable to handle pressure well, and thus experience burnout. Some workers have far greater stressors but effectively deal with them and avoid burnout. In this era, there is too much advancement in economic and industrial growth, fast lifestyles, increased work demand, too many expectations in a short period of time, and incompetent and unprofessional leadership running businesses without respect for human beings and their ability to perform work to match their skills. This leads to psychological stress, which later leads to exhaustion. Nowadays, economic values are greater than human values.

The most common factor leading to burnout is mismatch between the job, the person doing that job, and work overload. Doing too much with too few resources and going beyond personal limits may be due to downsizing. It is directly related to job demands and job resources. Job demands are the physical and psychological costs of work, such as work pressure and emotional demands. Burnout may be caused by job demand and job resources, which result in exhaustion and disengagement at work. Burnout is found in all kinds of jobs, and it has a similar presentation.

Physician Burnout

Burnout occurs among the highly educated, trained, and professional group we called physicians, who have become increasingly greater victims of burnout over the last few years. This increase in the incidences of burnout with suicide may be due to the advancement of fast-growing technologies in the medical field for which our older generation of physicians (including me) are slow to learn. Keeping up with these advancements includes needing more time to update patients' electronic medical records, and we do not have enough speed to complete the task within the given time frame as compared to the new generation of physicians, who are adept at using this technology and have been trained in this new electronic environment. In my opinion, this also could be a factor among our older generation, which leads to frustration and chronic stress and then advances to burnout.

It is my hope that this chapter will help you to determine whether you really are experiencing the onset of burnout and to imagine what exactly went wrong with your thinking process for burnout to develop. The scope of this book will provide a platform for physician burnout victims to come together to narrow down the real cause of burnout as a common factor to all, which will make it easier to find a final, effective treatment solution at both the individual and the organizational levels. It is important that organizations also realize they must play a role in treating burnout victims to prevent suicide in the future. Psychiatrists and psychologists must work together to eliminate the mental health stigma for these victims so that they may once again be beneficial to society as physicians. I believe that this is possible if we are sincere in helping burnout victims by treating their depression and suicidal thoughts and by returning them to mainstream life. In this way, we will help not only physicians but also their entire families.

Workplace burnout happens for a many of reasons, and various organizations have failed to keep it from occurring in spite of spending a lot of revenue to do just that. Statistics show that the physician burnout and suicide rates are constantly increasing. When I learned this, I immediately decided to write a book. In my thirty-seven years of professional life, I went through various stressors, exhaustion, and frustrations, as is common for anyone. I noticed that all these factors began to affect my daily work performance, and I started to have decreased motivation to accomplish tasks. Fortunately, I thought about my internal changes and started analyzing how I could eliminate these negative feelings before they became chronic. I also realized that I needed to gain control of my negative thinking.

In this universe, everything is created in pairs, which is the combination of opposites, such as males and females or positive and negative. The pairing or parity phenomenon is also well-known in molecular genetics, as in examples of the double helical structure of DNA and the composition of double-stranded RNA molecules. This parity can be seen in our understanding of physics, where there is a duality known as matter and antimatter. Recently researchers have tried to broaden their understanding of burnout to focus on positive antithesis (which is a positive state identified as engagement) to counter disengagement as a symptom of burnout and try to treat burnout by providing incentives, such as employee appreciation. The goal is to help employees come out of the negativity of disengagement and return to normal life with renewed energy to tackle new challenges at work.

Similarly, we are psychologically composed of negative and positive thinking, we are either convergent or divergent thinkers. We have the ability to adopt the right pathway to correct ourselves from negativity. This is important because everyone has weaknesses, which can develop negativity in people. You should accept the negative aspects of yourself but also focus on how you can improve the positives of a situation.

My mind was compelled to accept the reality that burnout was happening among a highly educated professional class of people, and we did not have any effective solutions for this issue. I started thinking outside the box and put myself in the shoes of a physician who was suffering from early symptoms of burnout, was going through real burnout, or was suffering from depression with suicidal thoughts due to worthlessness. I decided to put my mind under those circumstances and create stress within myself while developing an acceptable solution to this issue without the need for financial resources. As human beings, we are a very adaptable species. We have an ability to adapt and survive under adverse circumstances.

First, I decided to think about any episodes of real burnout during my thirty-eight-year career, and I recalled several occasions when I was overwhelmed and under a lot of stress. In this instance, I worked at a psychiatric hospital from November 1985 to December 1988 as an attending physician and pulmonologist to exclude medical illness from psychiatric illness. In this capacity, I had to learn about psychiatric illnesses, human psychology, human behavior, and various types of personalities. In the beginning, it was hard to clearly understand this new field of medicine. If I did not have control of this area, then I could not differentiate psychiatric illness from medical illness. It was an art to learn fast; I could not continue in this job unless I demonstrated this skill as soon as possible. I knew I started this job with minimal knowledge about psychiatry and with no skill to diagnose. Because of my own interests, I was curious to see whether I could quickly learn about this new field. It was a challenge for me, and I wanted to see whether I had hidden potential talents and skill sets in this field. I spent extra effort reading about various diagnosed cases by the hospital psychiatrist and trying to match the clinical symptoms under the diagnosed condition, which helped me to understand and provide a foundation for various psychiatric illnesses. If I failed to understand psychiatric illnesses and their progress with identifying serious adverse effects of prolonged use of antipsychotic drugs, then it would be impossible to see the conditions as relevant to an underlying medical illness. Learning new things in the beginning is always a challenge for anyone unless we are intrinsically motivated to handle situations for their own merit. This helps to gain confidence in your future career to prevent early burnout. During this phase, I was also frustrated and under stress. But I learned that if I wanted to survive in a highly stressful environment, I had to modify my survival strategies. This thinking provided me with a new dimension to survive and has resulted in many achievements throughout my career. I learned how to prevent burnout.

After six months, I developed a very good understanding of psychiatry as a subject and could diagnose various psychiatric illnesses, such as anxiety, depression, mood disorder, schizophrenia, and drug abuse, as well as how to manage antipsychotic medication side effects. Now, after several years of experience, observation, and developing skills to self-analyze, I have a better understanding of the human mind behind those negative or positive thoughts. From time to time, I started making adjustments in myself to reduce negativity toward life, which had a strong positive effect on my professional career. In the process, I started feeling satisfied and happy toward life, the world, my family, and all human beings. Now I am ready to teach our professional colleagues how they can change their negative thinking to positive thinking and gain more positive energy. Then they will once again enjoy a happy life and a happy work environment. Every negative event has a positive aspect hidden in it. You must always keep hope; there is always a chance. Always be grateful for what you have. For example, if you are struggling to pay your mortgage, there are always options, such as refinancing and revising your monthly budget. Everything is based on priorities and understanding the things you truly need versus the things you can do without.

This book is written to illustrate the journey to becoming a successful professional who can avoid burnout and become a strong leader with clear vision, thoughtfulness, and decision-making skills, all without fear of failure at any level of life. I provided you with a tool to evaluate your potential risk of burnout in the beginning of this book. You can convert this knowledge into a very strong professional career. The internal happiness you develop will allow you to once again love your life, love your work, and love your family. My book will help to inspire you to be a strong professional and to become a successful physician. I believe that if you adopt my remedy, then you will be able to correct your weaknesses and negativity of mind and to be free from burnout. If you want to be a true professional, then you should be optimistic, selfless, and not seek external rewards or glory. Instead, seek a sense of internal satisfaction and happiness, which is key to a successful life and essential for preventing burnout.

Those in the medical profession are fully aware of the extent of workplace burnout. They are required to develop skills to cope with the onset of burnout by identifying its precipitating causes: work-related stress. In my experience and observation, people with symptoms of burnout is fully aware of the precipitating factors that lead to their burnout, but it is possible that they are in the early phase rather than in the denial phase, brushing off any idea that there may be a problem that needs to be resolved. Here, I will connect a more recent study that showed that nearly seven thousand physicians using the Maslach Burnout Inventory (MBI). The study found that 54.4 percent of those surveyed reported at least one symptom of burnout.[10] This helps us identify the cause of burnout, take responsibility to find a solution, and avoid the friction that causes negative thinking about the work environment.

---

[10] Tait D. Shanafelt, Omar Hasan, Lotte N. Dyrbye, Christine Sinsky, Daniel Satele, Jeff Sloan, and Colin P. West, "Changes in Burnout and Satisfaction with Work-Life Balance in Physicians and the General US Working Population between 2011 and 2014," *Mayo Clinic Proceedings* 90, no. 2 (2015): 1600–13.

This situation can be managed at the institutional level and at the individual level. Sometimes both are necessary to solve the question of burnout. It is always recommended that the organization take corrective actions to evaluate if it is responsible for causing employee burnout. For example, if physicians are not comfortable with typing their notes, then they must be allowed to hire a scribe. Organizations can implement a corrective action plan to help keep its employees burnout-free, healthy, and happy.

In the United States, 49 percent of physicians and 28 percent of other workers report burnout incidences due to chronic work stress, long work hours, and poor satisfaction with work-life balance.[11] Many physicians are now leaving the profession, seeking early retirement, or working part time. According to a Mayo Clinic study, 7 percent of physicians between the ages of twenty-nine and sixty-five considered suicide within the last twelve months, compared to 4 percent of other workers. Approximately four hundred doctors commit suicide each year. It is also challenging to understand the effect of physician burnout on patient care. It is important to bring burnout under control. We must act as early as possible.

The incidence of burnout is high among physicians. In 2015, for the first time, physician burnout was the leading health-care issue. In 2016, it was again a leading issue. The following statistics will provide a better understanding of the severity of the issue.

---

[11] Ibid. Other studies have found similar rates of burnout in the surgical specialties, including orthopedic, oncologic, cardiothoracic, and plastic surgery; see Karen E. Deveny, "Transition from Residency to Practice: Life Does Get Better!" *JAMA Surgery* 149, no. 9 (2014): 948–53; Charles M. Balch and Tait S. Shanafelt, "Dynamic Tension between Success in a Surgical Career and Personal Wellness: How Can We Succeed in a Stressful Environment and a 'Culture of Bravado'?" *Annals of Surgical Oncology* 18, no. 5 (2011): 1213–16; Omar A. Jarral, Kamran Baig, Kunal Shetty, and Thanos Athanasiou, "Sleep Deprivation Leads to Burnout and Cardiothoracic Surgeons Have to Deal with Its Consequences," *International Journal of Cardiology* 179 (2015): 70–72; and Christina Prendergast, Erika Ketteler, and Gregory Evans, "Burnout in the Plastic Surgeon: Implications and Interventions," *Aesthetic Surgery Journal* 37, no. 3 (2017): 363–68.

Results from the "Medscape Lifestyle Report 2016: Bias and Burnout" are based on responses from more than 15,800 doctors representing twenty-five specialties. The report provides the following conclusions.[12]

+ The burnout percentage across the twenty-five specialties represented in the survey ranges from 40 to 55 percent.

+ There is an increasing trend in bureaucratic tasks, spending too many hours on these tasks, and too much computer use in clinical practice.

+ Burnout is linked to patient bias. The report focused on bias and burnout as two key factors affecting physicians' personal lives. Noting depersonalization as an aspect of physician burnout, the report identified a correlation between higher rates of burnout and greater bias toward patients.

+ Women are more burned out than men. "Though the rates of burnout have trended upward for both men and women in previous years, women seem to be affected by burnout more. Fifty-five percent of women and 46 percent of men surveyed reported burnout. And although men and women reported nearly identical levels of happiness at home (60% and 59%, respectively), only 26% of the women surveyed reported feeling happy at work compared to 33% of men."

Physician burnout may have an effect on patient care, including the physicians themselves. Medical residents and medical students are taking it very seriously. I am afraid that if the causes of physician burnout are not addressed properly, then in the near future, there will be a serious shortage of physicians compared to the growing elderly population in the United States. I have noticed that the general US population is reluctant to go into the medical field due to the cost

---

[12] Carol Peckham, "Medscape Lifestyle Report 2016: Bias and Burnout," Medscape, updated January 13, 2016, www.medscape.com/slideshow/lifestyle-2016-overview-6007335#18.

of becoming a physician and the associated debt; physician suicides would also make people think twice before entering the field. Even medical students and medical residents are committing suicide prior to become physicians. The bottom line is that there is a limited attraction to becoming a physician.

All physicians know that one day they may develop burnout due to exhaustion, depersonalization, lack of efficacy, and loss of compassion. Clinical practice as a doctor in any field is a high-demand, high-pressure, and stressful environment, with very little ability to maintain energy and compassion. All medical specialties have different challenges, such as working long hours as surgeons, or administrative issues such as insurance reimbursement in the family practice clinic. There is no real life for doctors who work long hours. It is a challenge for most doctors to balance life and work, which can drain their physical and emotional energy.

I believe that we are not providing proper guidelines to prepare medical students for the future hardships they will face as doctors, including performing noble duties to serve humanity with high efficiency and with strong internal happiness. I have heard from various medical students that studying is tough but that once they become doctors, it will be easier because they will have more wealth. This is the wrong approach because the real practical life begins with various loan debts, long work hours, less time with patients, keeping careful tabs on patient medical records to prevent future lawsuits, fulfilling organizational expectations, and lacking time to spend with family and friends. All this can lead to emotional and physical exhaustion, bringing more negativity into physicians' lives and initiating the early onset of burnout. When you become a doctor, you take an oath to serve humanity, which is the most important thing to keep in mind. Be ready to sacrifice your time, money, and sleep for your patients. This knowledge will help to keep alive your intrinsic motivation and avoid draining all your positive energy, which will prevent burnout. At the same time, we need strong, honest, and sincere hospital leadership to develop friendly, helpful work environments that will boost the morale, respect, and confidence of doctors and other staff to prevent future burnout. A disconnect or gap between a doctor's personality and the job's demand will erode the doctor's confidence, ambition, and motivation, which leads to stress and reduced job performance.

Physician burnout is becoming more prevalent. It is the responsibility of medical educators to communicate with students a need to balance their future expectations. As they advance in their careers, the hurdles and challenges they will encounter can be managed only by having a positive attitude and good personal energy to achieve their long-term goals of success, including a happy personal life as well as the ability to provide quality care to patients by giving them hope to survive with positive thinking.

In my experience, if doctors engage in positive thinking and help dying patients believe they are true fighters, then patients will also come under their positive energy zone, which will give them a new hope to survive longer. It is human nature that no one wishes to die young. For example, I had a patient with left leg gangrene due to snake bite three weeks prior. He was not receiving proper treatment because he lived in a remote, underserved area. This patient was a thirty-six-year-old farmer, and the surgeon wanted to amputate at the knee level. The surgeon was in a hurry, fearing that the spread of gangrene could cause death. I was on call as the attending physician. The patient was badly infected. It was easy to grant permission for the amputation surgery, but I am a true fighter, and I wanted to save his leg. I spoke to the patient with hope and confidence, and I asked permission from him to treat his wound. I asked him to trust me and to give me forty-eight hours to see if improvement occurred or if further deterioration would necessitate amputation. The patient was depressed about losing his leg and wondered how he would support his family in the future. With my intervention, the patient received some hope that his leg might be saved. He looked directly into my eyes and sensed my positive energy and enthusiasm to manage the gangrene and save his leg from amputation. I had faith and confidence that it would respond to my treatment. It was a great surprise that after forty-eight hours, healing was noted at the periphery of wound, and the patient was fully recovered in twelve days. His leg was saved. As a doctor, it was my happiest day to serve humanity in a true sense in the spirit of the oath I took at the time of my medical graduation.

I share this example to inspire physicians to keep healthy, positive memories alive at all times. This gives you energy to better serve humanity and feel proud to be a good doctor who helps suffering patients—people who look to their doctors to find cures for their illnesses. If doctors take a positive approach in their own lives, then they can learn to survive under difficult working environments and to maintain a positive outcome. Anyone can perform well in excellent work conditions. We need to train our supervisors, managers, bosses, and CEOs to know when, according to employees' behavior and job performance, they are showing symptoms of early burnout. If employees are not performing well and are unable to meet deadlines, then it means they might have underlying burnout. So far, all questionnaires were generated for research, not for family physicians to screen patients and evaluate early burnout.[13]

In my opinion, it is not possible for burnout victims to become burnout-free without engaging in self-analysis to understand what triggered the burnout. It takes serious effort to find a disconnect between expectation and reality and then to change weaknesses into strengths. On the other hand, people with burnout symptoms can focus on achieving small tasks, which will lead to gains in their self-confidence and abilities. This can further motivate them to accept bigger challenges. Accomplishing these tasks will help them identify hidden talents and skill sets and improve their job competence. These talents and skill sets can provide them with long-term stability in the

---

[13] Robert Nagler Miller, "Measure, Act on These 6 Factors Tied to Physician Burnout," AMA Wire, April 24, 2017, https://wire.ama-assn.org/life-career/measure-act-these-6-factors-tied-physician-burnout.

workplace and perhaps even raise them to a higher position in the organization as a leader.

By accomplishing tasks on a daily basis, practice will make you perfect. Very soon you will no longer feel stressed, exhausted, and frustrated. You can feel pleasure while living in a new environment with your positive energy. You may enter into an uninterrupted state of flow when working on your tasks as a physician or as any other professional because you are fully absorbed in your work, and you are not paying attention to any factors external to those tasks, such as lack of resources. You will have to learned how to give your all. Once you return from this state, you feel a sense of pleasure that invigorates you, allowing you to use your unique skill sets to tackle additional projects. Repeat this process on a daily basis without complaining about lack of resources or about administrators or managers whose lack of cooperation does not allow you to perform your duties. These are all related to negative thinking. Eliminate this bad habit. Don't complain; instead, focus only on your work and how you can perform the best in the worst situations. In my personal experience, this is the only way to succeed in your career.

I worked as a physician in Pakistan and Saudi Arabia with limited resources. When questions arose related to patient safety, I never compromised with hospital administration. Later in this book, I will share with you my experience of taking immediate actions to let hospital administrators know that I am a physician, that I am responsible, and that I took an oath to serve my patients with honesty and sincerity to reduce their suffering and pain and to improve their quality of life. It is a usual practice all over the world that the hospital administration tries to control physicians and put them under stress to earn business and generate revenue. Physicians must learn where the boundaries are to limit hospital administration. Administrators are generally not physicians, and they run the hospital as a corporate organization. The only way physicians can function well and stay long term in any organization is to earn respect and trust through hard work, honesty, and sincerity by meeting the organization's mission and vision. Once physicians reach this level, they have already crossed all the hurdles, and now the organization's leadership will be ready to listen to physicians' suggestions regarding resources for the betterment of patient care and enhancing the organization's reputation to earn more business. Now top leadership will be happy with you, and you will feel rewarded and will have achieved your expectations of internal satisfaction and contentment. Now you will be considered an asset for the organization. After this, you will be in a commanding situation in the hospital, and hospital administration will not dictate to you about cutting resources or put unnecessary pressure and stress on you as a physician. Physicians must be strong leaders in any health-care facility, be strong decision makers for patient care, and know how to convince hospital administration to do the right thing for the benefit of the patients.

Patients are able to best judge physician quality because they are the real stakeholders. In my clinical practice, managing patients in Pakistan and Saudi Arabia, almost all patients have the intuition to judge physicians about whether they look serious as they listen to the patient, take a step-by-step medical history, examine a patient to find clinical signs relevant to diagnosis, request relevant tests to further narrow down the correct diagnosis, and then develop a treatment plan to cure illness (or for incurable diseases, implement a treatment plan that will provide better pain and disease control). In this way, patients told me their physicians were good and were trying their best to treat them. This patient judgment and feeling will help patients to be in compliance with the treatment plan and schedule regular follow-up appointments for chronic conditions. Follow-up appointments help physicians treat patients who are not responding to a first line of treatment to think of other options to further manage their care or to refer them to a specialty physician for a new diagnosis. It will also provide continuing education for the physician through referral to another specialty. In this way, patients will develop additional trust in their physicians. This is the foundation of a long-lasting, good reputation for physicians. Patients are the best advertising tools for physicians and hospitals. They can boost morale and feelings of internal happiness that physicians are doing a good job and are really serving humanity. Patients with chronic illnesses are the best judges of physicians based on good or bad behavior, attitude, strong listening ability, patient eye contact, purposeful handshakes, and explaining the treatment plan in a way that patients can understand, which encourages good treatment compliance and follow-up. These actions will help patients gain confidence in their providers.

This trust allows physicians to place themselves in the patient's situation, who may be suffering from any disease, whether mild or serious. Many patients' immediate reaction could be negative thinking, believing that they could die from the disease, that it may not be cured, or that the medicine will not work. Physician selection is important for patients' treatment plans. If patients notice that the physician is mentally not paying attention to them, distracted by phones, talking with other staff present in the room, typing in the medical record without patient eye contact, failing to address concerns about whether to take medication, failing to do a proper exam, or deciding to wait on lab or radiology reports to make a diagnosis, then trust is not established between patients and physicians. I have noticed that some physicians' history-taking techniques and exams are not systematic. Physicians did not use their clinical judgment to clinch clinical diagnoses. If the wrong people join the medical field and become physicians, they may create trouble for patients and for themselves, which could lead to burnout. If physicians are interested in and passionate about their field, then long work hours and lack of time to spend with family will not generate stress because they are doing their best according to their professional responsibilities.

Today, in social gatherings or even at home, everyone is looking at their mobile phones, even when driving or eating. Some use the phone too much, looking at irrelevant messages to show other people that they are always very busy and have no time to care about others. Some people do not understand that these habits are damaging their social life or family life. I also notice in social gatherings that people will ask a general question, but once an answer is forthcoming, they immediately start playing with their phones. They are then totally distracted, and they leave the other person frustrated. I started reducing contact with those people. People who are doing this are harming themselves, not me. The advantage of social gatherings is to share issues and problems in the hopes of gaining good solutions and increasing knowledge. This wisdom can then be shared with others, motivating them in turn, which will help to reduce various stressors and frustrations by getting guidance from close, sincere, and honest friends. Friendship must be beneficial, with selection of comparatively positive thinkers who will give you positive energy. You will be able to feel that you are attracted to and under the protective cover of the positive thinker's electromagnetic force. Your heart and mind will think in positive directions. This is the beginning of positive development. If you are socializing with a negative thinker and engaging in depressive talk, then you will acquire more negativity. That will further increase your stress and frustration, moving you toward burnout.

My philosophy is not to interfere in the personal lives of my family and friends by calling to ask how they are. They may be busy doing important work, and calling unnecessarily interrupts them. In my opinion, it is a luxury in the United States to use free calling services. People do not know they are wasting several hours a day by talking and oversaturating their memory cells with backbites, provoking talk that incites one another, increasing negativity in society, and creating more misunderstandings among people instead of generating more motivation. It is my observation that negative thinkers are drawn to other like-minded people—that is, other negative thinkers. I noted that they feel happier during talk with like-minded people because both are seeking sympathy. If I am positive thinker, and I try to tell them to correct their negativity, then sometimes they become angry with me because they do not want to correct themselves. They believe that because I do not have negative thoughts, I will not understand. However, others have listened to my logical explanations, and they corrected themselves and became positive thinkers. People must decide whether they want to correct themselves and have the sweet taste of success.

If I am sitting in an office to wait for an appointment or am traveling in car, train, or airplane, I do not want to see my phone or e-mail. I don't even want to read a book because these occasions are blessings for me to relax and imagine beautiful moments of my life or any occasion made memorable to me. It is my great relaxation time. After this, I get up with new ideas and thoughts to accomplish my remaining daily targets to achieve more happiness. I tune my body and mind accordingly. During weekends, each day I have eight to ten targets to achieve. This allows me to feel pleasure and happiness at the end of the day and to be ready for Monday with ambition to tackle new accomplishments at work. In my experience, too much negative thinking is the source of reduced energy, motivation, and self-confidence, which are the major hindrances to your success.

Do whatever task you are doing, but do it with compassion, full attention, and focus. By doing this, you will achieve an optimum experience and add a new skill set, which will increase your confidence and intrinsic motivation. Train yourself to do more and more work to achieve your goals, Always be ready to accept new challenges; no one will defeat you. You will feel like Superman as you accept and finish challenges with positive outcomes. You will generate positive energy; like an electromagnetic force, people will be attracted to you and will want to listen to you to get the benefits of your positive energy. Try to make friends with positive thinkers, not with negative and obsessive people who will destroy your energy. It is very simple to diagnose a negative thinker. Anyone with negative thoughts will start a conversation with a complaint. That person never learns how to be happy and satisfied. In the past, from time to time I also had negative thoughts and fears of the future, failure, or an unsuccessful career. Later in this book, I will explain how I deleted negative thoughts from my mind and converted to more positive thinking.

This book offers a further understanding of burnout in the hopes of providing guidance to those who are seeking to become burnout-free. This book is as much an exploration of burnout as it is my personal experience. I implemented various principles to reduce stress and frustration, and I applied them through several techniques while living in Pakistan, Saudi Arabia, and the United States.

Conclusion

Burnout is a genuine issue that can lead to devastating personal and professional consequences. Doctors with burnout cannot provide quality care to patients, and it increases the chance of medical errors, poor decision making, hostile attitudes toward patients, and difficult relationships with coworkers. It is a global phenomenon. Physicians belong to a highly vulnerable group for experiencing burnout due to multiple stressors and an increased risk of anxiety and depression, poor sleep, misuse of alcohol and drugs, and difficult marital relationships.

The general workplace population, and particularly physicians, must show flexibility or quick adaptability to overcome stress. Employers must try to provide a healthy, stress-free work environment so that employees can achieve work-life balance and enjoy job security while preventing burnout. Once the burnout process has started, then a psychological consultation is needed to begin cognitive behavioral therapy and learn relaxation techniques. At the same time, cooperation is required from employers to improve the work environment. Prevention is always better than treatment when it comes to burnout. The extent of burnout may vary depending on the practice setting, specialty, and changing work environment. An understanding of dynamic risk factors associated with burnout may help to prevent and treat burnout. Physicians can recover from burnout because they are professional and understand their own psychology, allowing for a quick recovery from precipitating stressful situations. There is no need to quit or change jobs or to think about early retirement if you are self-motivated to accept burnout as a challenge: you know how you can overcome it, or you can seek advice from a psychologist or psychiatrist.

Physicians in many countries are experiencing great frustration in practicing medicine due to limited resources and corporate micromanagement of health-care delivery, media reports of medical errors, and unethical physician conduct. Patients challenge physicians' authority and skills. Patients also challenge other health-care-related providers, such as insurance companies.

I believe that burnout and stress management topics should be included in college and university curricula targeting medical students, residents, and practicing physicians to improve psychological well-being, professional career enjoyment, and the quality of care provided to patients.

One way to overcome the epidemic of burnout at the organizational level is to create an "Employee Burnout Prevention Questionnaire" drop box that is kept in a prominent area in the organization. The human resources department collects the questionnaires weekly to immediately identify employees who may develop burnout symptoms. A sample questionnaire is given at the end of the chapter as a suggestion. The department supervisor and managers must be trained to find ways to evaluate early employee burnout.

If employees have had one or more symptoms of burnout, then they need to contact the supervisor for information on how it can be prevented. Employers must listen to the employee and manage the concern.

Supervisor or Manager's Early Assessment of Employee Burnout

Supervisor or Manager's Assessment	Strongly Disagree	Disagree	Neutral	Agree	Strongly Agree	Response
Employee's inability to manage day-to-day activities	1	2	3	4	5	
Employee looks under pressure at work	1	2	3	4	5	
Employee is taking long time to complete task	1	2	3	4	5	
Employee struggles to meet deadlines	1	2	3	4	5	
Employee is unable to meet high job demands due to poor control	1	2	3	4	5	
There are high expectations at work, and the employee is unable to meet the constant demands at work	1	2	3	4	5	
Employee is missing deadlines due to forgetfulness	1	2	3	4	5	
Employee has a mismatch of job skill set	1	2	3	4	5	

	1	2	3	4	5	
Employee has a lack of enthusiasm and motivation	1	2	3	4	5	
Employee productivity at work is decreasing	1	2	3	4	5	
Employee regularly calls in sick	1	2	3	4	5	
Employee interest at work is decreasing	1	2	3	4	5	
Employee shows irritability	1	2	3	4	5	
Employee hates his or her job	1	2	3	4	5	
Employee does not care about work while at the job	1	2	3	4	5	

Scoring: < 30 = Not burned out; 30–60 = Would welcome a few changes at work; > 60 = Early phases of burnout, needing corrective action to prevent late onset of burnout.

The Role of Primary Care Physician Screening for Burnout Victims

There is no internationally accepted definition of burnout. I will try to define what I felt as an early victim of burnout.

Burnout is a dysfunctional or maladaptive state of mind where employees cannot meet the expectations of the work environment. It presents as a progression that cannot be identified by laboratory tests or diagnostic imaging. It is a huge problem in the world when expectations outstrip reality. Individual personalities, attitudes, and behaviors presenting as severe emotional, psychological, and physical exhaustion due to negative attitudes toward the workplace are interconnected with life events, including apprehension, tension, pressure, forgetfulness, and overwhelming situations. It poses socioeconomic consequences and mental health stigmas.

As a physician, I used the following diagnostic criteria to identify and successfully manage approximately fifty cases of early burnout victims, all without medication. I provided one-on-one consultation to find the potential cause of the onset of burnout symptoms. An individualized self-care guide applied various solutions to help these victims become burnout-free in the future. Most victims responded well in six months to one year, depending on their personalities and attitudes. In my experience, burnout victims are negative thinkers who tend to obsess. It takes time to help them develop positive attitudes toward the workplace. Time is key to curing early burnout victims without emotional scars so that they can return to normal, healthy, and successful lives.

Consider this example. A forty-year-old male CEO in an engineering company came to me for consultation after a recent onset of flu for three days. In addition to taking his history, during which I learned he had been a heavy smoker for twenty years, examination findings correlated with chronic obstructive pulmonary disease with acute exacerbation. As a pulmonologist, I decided to spend time with the patient and encourage him to quit smoking in order to prevent future complications of the disease. I drew a diagram of the lungs and explained the multiple complications of smoking. I also read the patient's facial expressions to determine how far he was willing to take my advice to quit smoking. I asked for more detail regarding his smoking habit, and it became clear that the number of packs had increased over the years. now he was a chain-smoker. Right away, this gave me a clue that he might be suffering from some job-related stress due to holding a higher position. I decided to take his occupational history. He had a higher degree in engineering and held a decision-making position. He was used to working late and felt physical and emotional exhaustion. He looked physically tired, as though he was under too much stress. I remembered that he had almost all the symptoms related to early burnout (discussed later in this chapter). The most important thing I noticed was that this patient realized that the doctor was taking the time to sincerely try to help him. My work became easy, and my first task for this patient was for him to quit smoking. I saw an immediate response from him, along with a positive attitude. He threw out his cigarette packet and lighter and gladly told me that he would no longer smoke. He was determined, and he did it.

I discussed the next level of managing his early burnout, because the patient was fully motivated and in listening mode. It is my experience that once someone is fully charged with intrinsic motivation, my work as a physician is easy. A doctor's sincerity builds the doctor-patient relationship on faith, leading to good results from treatment compliance, which improves quality of life in the long run. It helped that in addition to being an attending internal medicine physician and pulmonologist, I also have experience in treating all kind of psychiatric patients. For this patient, I started with reassurance that if he would follow my advice to manage his workplace stress by keeping his self-motivation alive, splitting daily tasks into smaller units, and feeling happy after completing each task, he would build confidence in himself. He would then begin to develop clarity of mind for how to deal with bigger projects while ensuring a high success rate. After each success, it is natural to feel happy, gain more positive energy, and cultivate a freshness of new ideas to brighten your professional career.

I followed up with him for one year before I migrated to the United States. I met with him prior to leaving Pakistan, and he was no longer smoking and was fully burnout-free. I am still in contact with him, and he is doing great without any health issues.

After diagnosing and treating several burnout patients, I developed a clinical intuition to identify workplace stress through patients' facial expressions. Using this intuition, I've inquired about patients' workplace performance. Immediately, they opened up to me and told me that they had moderate to severe burnout. I provided them with self-care solutions to reduce their workplace stresses. One started working from home to free himself from workplace stress, and he was able to control the early onset of burnout.

Symptoms related to the *early onset* of burnout include the following.

1. The employee frequently calls in sick.
2. The employee thinks about early retirement.
3. The employee is unable to manage day-to-day activities.
4. The employee struggles to meet deadlines.
5. The employee misses deadlines due to forgetfulness.
6. The employee lacks enthusiasm and motivation.
7. The employee feels overwhelmed.
8. The employee feels that the workplace saps energy.
9. The employee takes a long time to complete a task.
10. The employee has a mismatch between skill and job.

Symptoms related to the *late onset* of burnout include the following.

1. The employee has lost the purpose to survive.
2. The employee feels like there is nothing more to give.

3. The employee no longer feels satisfaction or a sense of accomplishment.
4. The employee feels alone in the world.
5. The employee feels overloaded and unappreciated.
6. The employee feels worthless, exhausted, and frustrated.
7. The employee suffers from depression symptoms, including extreme fatigue, loss of passion, and intensifying cynicism (feelings of ineffectiveness).
8. The employee feels helpless, hopeless, cynical, and resentful.
9. The employee feels the hallmarks of burnout, including exhaustion, cynicism, and inefficiency.
10. The employee has suicidal thoughts.

Burnout is a difficulty in life management characterized by vital exhaustion. The symptoms of vital exhaustion include two weeks of daily experience of decreased energy, difficulty concentrating, irritability, emotional instability, dizziness, and sleep difficulty in addition to interfering with patients' capacity to perform their work responsibilities.

For burnout victims, ideally, they could follow up with a family physician who can screen for and identify burnout. It is also important that employees' supervisors or managers identify early burnout victims and refer them to their family physicians for further evaluation. If employees think that the workplace environment is provoking burnout, then employers must take corrective measures to halt further progression of severe burnout in their employees by providing some supervision or changing departments according to work experience so that employees feel comfortable in accomplishing daily tasks with gaining confidence.

High expectations always outstrip reality, which leads to loss of purpose to survive as well as negative thoughts and obsession. Life is full of situational stresses that may be beyond our control. These stresses may start with conflicts between values or with a mismatch between experience and skill. It is multifactorial and multidimensional because burnout victims have their own belief systems. Burnout victims engage in excessive negative thinking, which is very painful for them and generates fear, loss of confidence, and confusion surrounding the achievement of daily tasks. We must teach people how to reduce stress with positive thinking so that they can become burnout-free by seeing a psychologist or psychiatrist.

In my opinion, many people have undiagnosed burnout that could lead to negative outcomes for society in terms of productivity. More frequent psychological evaluations can prevent burnout. There must be no mental health stigma associated with these kinds of evaluation. There must be more training of psychiatrists and psychologists to evaluate people's personality types, behaviors, and attitudes to reduce future burnout incidences. If negative thought patterns are identified, positive thinking or proper treatment can be prescribed. It can lead to success in both work and family life. Problems with personality, behavior, and attitude that are successfully resolved with this method can lead to improvement at the societal level and in the workplace.

Burnout victims must ask for help to seek the best advice and moral support. Try to learn how to manage stress. Discuss specific concerns with an appropriate colleague, supervisor, or manager to find the best solution, such as flexible work hours or teaming with a mentor to improve work performance. If there is an attitude issue, it must be corrected. You must find ways to stay relaxed and happy in order to improve performance. Try to control unreasonable and unrealistic demands. Learn how to avoid work-related stress, even if that means looking for another job that brings happiness and to which you are better suited. Learn to balance or control negative feelings to move toward a positive attitude, which will protect you from emotional exhaustion. Further interventions will depend on individual needs and may include relaxation techniques, counseling or psychotherapy, or antidepressant treatment by a referral to a psychiatrist. The following screening tool will help primary care physician easily diagnose early or late onset of burnout.

Primary Care Physician Screening Tool for Early Diagnosis of Burnout Victims

This tool will also be helpful for physicians themselves to find early burnout.

Family Physician Burnout Screening Assessment	Strongly Disagree	Disagree	Neutral	Agree	Strongly Agree	Response
Inability to manage day-to-day activities	1	2	3	4	5	
Feeling tension and pressure at work	1	2	3	4	5	
Long working hours.	1	2	3	4	5	
Struggle to meet deadlines	1	2	3	4	5	
High job demand and low control	1	2	3	4	5	
High expectations at work; unable to meet the constant demands at work	1	2	3	4	5	
Missing deadlines due to forgetfulness	1	2	3	4	5	
Mismatch of skill set and job activities	1	2	3	4	5	

	1	2	3	4	5	
Lack of enthusiasm and motivation	1	2	3	4	5	
Feeling overwhelmed	1	2	3	4	5	
Emotionally drained and unable to relax	1	2	3	4	5	
Taking a long time to complete tasks	1	2	3	4	5	
Decreased productivity at work	1	2	3	4	5	
Taking days off or regularly calling sick	1	2	3	4	5	
Lack of interest at work	1	2	3	4	5	
Technological issues at work, or lack of resources	1	2	3	4	5	
Expectation fails to meet reality	1	2	3	4	5	
No recognition	1	2	3	4	5	
Irritation	1	2	3	4	5	
Lack of energy at work	1	2	3	4	5	

Scoring: < 30 = Not burned out; 30–60 = Would welcome a few changes at work > 60 = Early phases of burnout; need corrective action to prevent late onset of burnout. Consult a primary care physician.

Primary Care Physician Screening Tool for Late Onset of Burnout Victims

This tool will also be helpful for physicians themselves to find late onset burnout.

Family Physician Burnout Screening Assessment	Strongly Disagree	Disagree	Neutral	Agree	Strongly Agree	Response
Negativity of workplace controls the mind	1	2	3	4	5	
Feelings of worthlessness, exhaustion, and frustration	1	2	3	4	5	
Depression, extreme fatigue, loss of passion, helplessness, and hopelessness	1	2	3	4	5	
Feeling tired and muscle aches	1	2	3	4	5	
No more feelings of satisfaction or accomplishment	1	2	3	4	5	
Feeling of ineffectiveness; cynicism	1	2	3	4	5	
Feeling of being overloaded and underappreciated	1	2	3	4	5	
Feeling isolation and emptiness inside	1	2	3	4	5	
Feeling like there is nothing more to give	1	2	3	4	5	
Feeling alone in the world	1	2	3	4	5	

Conflicts between your values and work place	1	2	3	4	5
Mismatch between experience and skill	1	2	3	4	5
Expectation is outstripped by reality	1	2	3	4	5
Feelings of paranoia at work	1	2	3	4	5
Effort-reward imbalance	1	2	3	4	5
Inefficiency at work	1	2	3	4	5
Excessive use of alcohol and drugs	1	2	3	4	5
Insomnia	1	2	3	4	5
Suicidal thoughts	1	2	3	4	5
Failed or unsuccessful attempt at suicide	1	2	3	4	5

Scoring: 0–50 = Beginning of late onset of burnout; need aggressive measures to stop progression. Consult PCP or psychologist; 51–100= Advanced phases of burnout; need immediate treatment from psychiatrist to prevent suicide and treat depression.

Chapter 4

Am I Burned Out at Work?

The eyes are a reflection of the heart and mind. If you are passionate about your work or about anything, then I can read your mind and heart through your eyes. It is very bright and deep, a feeling of talking to an intelligent person. Your interest in the issues under discussion shows, and sometimes we can understand silent messages that are reflected through the eyes that help us assess the needs of others. When you first begin working, these things are reflected when you are happy with your job. However, when you are unhappy with your job, your eyes are dull and tired. You are uninterested in your surroundings due to an underlying fear of losing your job, and you are self-occupied.

The signs of burnout are not only intrinsic but also extrinsic. Your facial expression is also important when diagnosing various phases of the psychological process going on in your mind or the nature of mental illness, depression, anxiety, drug abuse, intoxication, and various medical illnesses. Body gestures and language make up the whole of our appearance.

I used to diagnose early cases of burnout using my clinical intuition just by looking at patients' faces, eyes, and body language. Even before I spoke to these patients, I would know their mental well-being. Their expressions said it all. For instance, I met a worker and could tell just by his face and his eyes that he was overwhelmed. I started a conversation with him about his job, and he immediately admitted to me that he was in the early phases of burnout. First I listened to him, and then I confronted his thinking, which was negative. I knew that if he kept going in this direction, he would develop burnout. I explained how he could keep himself more positive by suggesting that he find pleasure in his work and not confront his boss. This would avoid establishing a shoddy work relationship that would do more harm than good. I decided to continue to follow up on his work environment and how he should tackle his work to be more productive and positive. After following my recommendations and making some changes at work, he is now happy and burnout-free.

Before defining burnout, I would like to introduce the idea of brownout, a close cousin of burnout. Burnout is everywhere, especially in the corporate world, where it is known as brownout. Brownout results from a mild form of burnout characterized by disengagement, discontent, lethargy, lack of motivation, and loss of interest related to job performance. It normally affects those over the age of thirty-five. Workers gradually lose interest in developing or hearing new ideas, and they reduce social activity and communication. They become withdrawn, and their main motivation is earning money in exchange for working long hours. This coexists with the inability to meet challenges or to complete tasks. With brownout, there is no loss of productivity, so it is a less severe version of burnout. Burnout is when we take something like this to its logical conclusion.

According to my thinking, burnout is a dysfunctional state of mind wherein one cannot meet the expectations of the work environment. It affects many professionals across the board. The onset of burnout is insidious, and one often does not realize it until a suicide attempt or other negative outcome occurs. Burnout leads to people missing work or loss of work. Ironically, professionals such as doctors and nurses work to heal others, but they do not take care of themselves, which leads to burnout. They are unable to cope with stress and do not consider that they are doing something good for suffering people—that they are keeping their patients' internal motivation alive and continuing their feelings of internal happiness.

Understanding Burnout

Burnout is the result of workplace stress. People use many terms to express burnout: frazzled, lassitude, tiredness, weariness, bleary, bushed, drained, jaded, knackered, limp, logy, breakdown, consumption, dullness, brain fog, mental exhaustion, emotional or mental collapse, and nervous exhaustion.

Burnout begins with work-related overload and feelings of tension and pressure, which lead to emotional stress while dealing with coworkers or members of the public.

Burnout manifests as a decrease in freshness, strength, and energy. However, it can manifest differently in different occupations. Physicians may expect better compensation from work than someone who is working for minimum wage. This is due to a combination of factors, such as high educational debt, reduced autonomy, lack of enthusiasm and motivation, feelings of ineffectiveness, and cynicism. Burnout is a state of emotional, mental, and physical exhaustion that is caused by excessive and prolonged stress. It occurs when people feel overwhelmed, emotionally drained, and unable to meet constant work demands. As the stress continues, people lose interest or motivation to perform their jobs efficiently. Burnout begins with irritability. Once a feeling of burnout begins, it reduces productivity at work and saps energy, leaving feelings of helplessness, hopelessness, cynicism, and resentment. Eventually, burnout victims feel that they have nothing more to give.

Burnout starts with feeling overwhelmed and anxious. If these feelings are not addressed right away, they will have future consequences. Once you start feeling that you are dysfunctional, you are moving toward burnout. Exhaustion means a loss of motivation, which will cause distress and feelings of ineffectiveness leading to burnout. For me, the following factors can precipitate early burnout:

an unhealthy job environment, insufficient resources to perform the job, and a mismatch between job description and skill set. The unhappiness and detachment that burnout causes can threaten your job, your relationships, and your health.

But burnout can be overcome. There are plenty of things you can do to regain your balance and to start to feel positive and hopeful again. Psychological stress is the main cause of burnout. In most cases, three factors are involved in burnout: exhaustion (a hallmark of burnout), cynicism, and inefficacy.

Ninety percent of burnout workers meet the criteria for depression. Maslach and Leiter provided the antithesis of burnout by using the term *engagement*.[14] Engagement requires fulfilling the following three factors to avoid burnout.

+ Bring back energy by using self-motivation.
+ Keep involving yourself in positive activities at work in order to gain self-confidence.
+ Self-confidence leads to clarity in vision and goals. Achieving your targets results in a positive outcome and enhances your efficacy.

The Internal Feelings of Burnout Victims

Our workplace environments are highly unpredictable and constantly changing, which leads to feeling helpless, overloaded, or unappreciated. If you feel like this most of the time, then you may have burnout.

Burnout is a gradual process. The signs and symptoms are subtle at first, but they get worse as time goes on. Think of the early symptoms as red flags that something is wrong and must be addressed. If you pay attention and act to reduce your stress, you can prevent a major breakdown. Very early presentation of burnout includes feelings of

---

[14] Maslach, Christina, and Michael P. Leiter. "Understanding the Burnout Experience: Recent Research and Its Implications for Psychiatry." World Psychiatry, vol. 15, no. 2, 2016, pp. 103–111., doi:10.1002/wps.20311.

tiredness, muscle aches, headaches, changes in sleep and appetite patterns, decreased motivation, a sense of failure, feeling defeated or alone in the world, loss of feelings of satisfaction or accomplishment, an increasingly cynical and negative outlook, taking longer to complete tasks, taking out your frustration on others, taking days off, lack of interest at work, taking drugs and alcohol to cope, and withdrawing from all responsibilities and becoming more isolated. This means you have too much stress and are feeling pressured and gradually losing control. You have developed feelings of emptiness. If you are experiencing burnout, you have lost hope of positive changes in your situation.

Signs of early stress include feeling over-engaged, and followed by loss of energy, and anxiety, all of which may damage your health.

Signs of early burnout include disengagement, blunted emotions, no new ideas, no motivation, and feelings of hopelessness, helplessness, isolation, and detachment, which lead to depression and feeling that life is worthless. This can cause suicidal ideation and even a suicide attempt.

The root cause of burnout is embedded into your workplace. If you feel overworked and undervalued, then you are at higher risk of burnout.

The Beginnings of the Clinical Manifestation (Subjective Complaints) of Burnout

The earliest onset of burnout starts with forgetfulness and reduced attention and concentration. You will be unable to complete tasks on time, which gradually increases your workload and feelings of being overburdened. If at this time you are not consistent in your time management, then you will gradually lose the confidence to deal with your workload. Now you start missing deadlines at work and experience lethargy and fatigue, which are related to frustration and exhaustion. These early internal signs of burnout will develop into full-fledged burnout.

Clinical presentation means that future burnout victims start feeling various symptoms, which can be described in different ways according to the person's subjective feelings and educational level. You can self-evaluate your symptoms to self-diagnose burnout and start self-managing according to the leading cause of burnout.

The following feelings will manifest in burnout victims depending on the severity of the elements surrounding the workplace environment. Physical complaints (the beginning of stress) start with many vague feelings, including headache, dizziness, fainting, palpitations, chest pain, shortness of breath, and abdominal discomfort, along with frequent flu or colds due to a suppressed immune system. Early onset of anxiety starts with tension and worry, which leads to feeling overwhelmed and to early symptoms of burnout. Early onset of depression starts with mild sadness and sometimes hopelessness, followed by guilty feelings and worthlessness; at this point, you must consult a psychologist. Poor sleep and reduced appetite are also part of depression. Early onset of anger starts with interpersonal tension and irritability, followed by outbursts of anger and arguments at work and home. A psychological consultation is needed to eliminate the cause of anger and to facilitate advancement. The onset of losing interest at work and at home starts with a reduced desire to go to work, arriving late to work, avoiding taking on new tasks at work, losing interest in home activities, and losing feelings of internal happiness. Life seems to be boring. With the onset of negative thinking or a move toward pessimism, you are now seeing the world through dark glasses that show the worst aspects of things or make you believe that the worst will happen; this is when self-confidence for the future starts to fade. The onset of isolation starts with resistance to socializing with staff at work or with friends at home, causing you to avoid all social gatherings and other interactions with people. The onset of detachment and cynicism is a feeling of disconnect from the environment due to isolative behaviors, causing you to remove yourself from physical and emotional responsibilities at work or home; this often extends to neglecting responses to e-mails and telephone calls or calling in sick.

Cynicism leads to a distrust of others and starts as a negative feeling. Cynicism is derived from an ancient Greek philosopher who practiced "Cynics," meaning living a purposeful life in agreement with nature. People could gain happiness by rigorous training and living in a natural way by rejecting all conventional desires for wealth, power, sex, and fame. A loss of enjoyment or pessimism at first may present itself as negative self-talk and/or moving from a glass-half-full to a glass-half-empty attitude. At its worst, this may move beyond how you feel about yourself and extend to trust issues with coworkers and family members and a feeling that you can't count on anyone. The onset of ineffectiveness starts as a feeling of apathy or hopelessness and increased irritability as a part of depression, which further reduces productivity and increases poor job performance, leading to ineffectiveness, lack of accomplishment, feelings of apathy, and hopelessness. Increased irritability starts as you begin to feel ineffective, unimportant, and useless, and you develop an increasing sense that you're not able to do things as efficiently or effectively as you once did. In the early stages, this can interfere in personal and professional relationships; at its worst, it can destroy relationships and careers. The onset of feeling unable to accomplish any tasks or targets is a part of negative feelings and leads to poor job performance. If you are experiencing any of these signs, then you have already started the process of burnout.

This is the time to take these signs seriously and to consult a psychologist If you know your personal strengths and weaknesses, that can help you choose the right career, make good decisions, or even pull you back from the burnout process. If you are able to focus what you do around your personal strengths, then you have the chance to create something remarkable while making it look like it's almost effortless for you. Your biggest personal strength is what is easy for you and what is likely not easy for everyone else. This is what you do best and where your real talents lie. If you want to have a comfortable life, you should focus on using those strengths to the fullest because that's where you have a competitive advantage and where you can create the most value for other people.

Similar to knowing your personal values, knowing your strengths and weaknesses raises your self-awareness and gives you clarity. People who do not have these insights into their personal values immediately need reassurance, encouragement, and appreciation. In my opinion, vacation will not help these people because once they return, the backlog of work overwhelms them, triggering the stress that leads to burnout. There is something missing in these people. Their obsession and lack of self-confidence to perform their jobs will stay in their minds, even during vacation time, and they will not be able to relax. Effectively combating this way of thinking requires individualized psychotherapy and psychoanalysis. By identifying the missing element, these people have a chance to correct themselves. This book will address corrective methods through self-assessment and self-help to manage burnout.

Chapter 5

My Experience and Self-management of Burnout to Prevent Severe, Uncontrolled Burnout

In this chapter, I will provide examples from my career as I worked as an attending physician and pulmonologist in Pakistan and Saudi Arabia from 1980 to 1993.

Whether in Pakistan, Saudi Arabia, or the United States, I always begin a job by taking it as a serious challenge in life, working hard to meet employer expectations, and finding my hidden talent to perform well, gain experience, and add new information to my skill set so I can handle any situation with confidence. I have always been able to accept additional projects beyond my job description, even now. It keeps me intrinsically motivated to conclude a new project, and my regular job performance stays at a very high level with internal satisfaction and happiness. This gives me self-assurance that I am capable of doing any task with positive results by maintaining motivation to achieve my target 100 percent, which I have done on several occasions.

In Pakistan, in the beginning I started with various locum jobs at different family practice clinics. Whatever salary was decided between parties and job description, I honestly abided by my commitments. During my thirty-eight years of professional life, I've observed that no one sticks to one's job description 100 percent. In my case, there was always extra work and extra projects coming my way. We have to accept these because in my experience, these opportunities always opened the door to add a new skill set to my professional life, regardless of whether these tasks were relevant to my educational background. I never say no to any task anywhere, whether at work or at home. I cultivate a habit to take all challenges in life with a positive attitude in the hopes of helping others. In this way, I always kept myself away from negative thinking. Some patients would come toward the end of working hours at the clinic, but I never refused to see a patient, and I never asked for extra money for extra time. These family practice clinics were the most popular clinics due to the owner's physicians, who established powerful relationships with patients. Patients had a sense that they would get better treatment and management from the clinic.

These owners of clinic physicians were out of the country for vacation or personal treatment abroad. It was a huge challenge as a new physician just out of residency to run these clinics alone and manage various patients who presented with either acute or chronic illnesses. Nearly every day, I was overloaded and overwhelmed with patients. A negative thought came to my mind that at the time of my interview, the hiring physician told me that he would not be at the clinic, which would considerably reduce the flow of patients, and my salary was set accordingly. It was the employer's expectation, but I noticed that it was the opposite of what he had said. The number of patient visits to the clinic increased 35 percent due to my good history-taking technique, diagnosis, and treatment plan, which improved patient confidence in physicians due to an increased cure rate. I also provided medical education according to the patients' disease process and prognosis. This improved medication compliance and follow-up. Patients developed respect for me.

As we all know, it is not easy to earn respect because to get to that point, we have to tolerate and sacrifice our time and money. Respect will not be earned overnight; we have to do hard work with sincerity.

Imagine if you are respected by the management, your supervisor, friends, patients, and social group. In this way, you will feel that you have value as a human being in society. If you frequently say no to your bosses, telling them that additional work is not in your job description, then their respect for you will erode. My philosophy is that if anyone comes to me and suggests doing some additional projects, it means the person has confidence and faith in my ability to accomplish the work with a positive outcome. I know the boss will not ask someone who is not competent. It is the best opportunity for me to find my hidden talent and skill set.

Do not think about any external awards because if you do not get it, then negative thinking will start, which leads to frustration and later to burnout. In my personal experience, when I worked in a family practice in those clinics, the clinic-owning physician never offered me extra money to compensate me for the good job I did; he told me that I had seen a smaller number of patients. I was always good with record keeping, and I provided him with a list of patients whom I had treated. He had not expected this, but I learned my lesson at the beginning that whatever extra work you will do, owners will not acknowledge it with any extra money. Particularly in Pakistan, no one will give you extra money for extra work with good results.

From that day, I determined that I would have no expectation of my employer but that I would always try to help everyone, even the employer, to contribute to success. This attitude gave me self-confidence to find hundreds of hidden abilities and skill sets, which are unlimited and now contribute to my great success and respect. Since then, I have had no negative thinking, tension, pressure, or frustration related to the job environment. Therefore, I am burnout-free. I hope these examples help you find a way to prevent burnout. If you understand my philosophy, then it will be easier for you to tackle burnout with a positive approach. If you agree to do additional work but also think you will receive additional money for these services, your employer will not give you any incentive, and then you will become a victim of burnout. You have two solutions: either you look for a new job, or you do extra work on new projects to add to your skill set. If you choose the latter, once you are successful in this, in my experience, no boss or organization will neglect you for future promotions in the organization to grow further.

I moved to Saudi Arabia under the Ministry of Health (MOH) as an attending physician and pulmonologist on January 2, 1988. They contracted with me at 4,600 Saudi riyals per month, a low salary, because I did not have a postgraduate degree from the United States or Britain. I had two additional postgraduate degrees from Pakistan, but the MOH gave no credit in the form of a better salary. Other attendings who worked at the same hospital in the Department of Medicine and who had foreign degrees received a monthly salary of SR 30,000–36,000, according to their experience. When I explained my additional experience in psychiatry, the MOH was kind enough to increase my salary by SR 500 per month. Now my starting salary was SR 5,100 per month. I was very happy. In the beginning, I had the same job description as other foreign-qualified attending physicians in the Department of Medicine whose salaries were six times greater than mine, and I had additional responsibility as a pulmonologist. According to these disparities, I could start early burnout due to negative thinking if I started comparing myself to them. However, I had accepted this job, and I had a commitment to do my best in spite of increasing clinical patient workload. I would establish and run new clinics, such as the asthma clinic, diabetic clinic, diabetic club, brucella (infective condition by drinking unpasteurized milk) clinic, and internal medicine clinic. I'd see inpatients, and remain on call to see patients in the ER, provide consultation for inpatient medical emergencies, and consult to determine whether a patient was fit for anesthesia before going into surgery.

My inpatient admission and clinic patient flow was high compared to the other three attending physicians. For example, from January 1988 to September 1993, I managed approximately sixty-five thousand patients. One can image my workload. I accepted this job as a challenge to serve in an Arabic-speaking nation even though I was unable to speak Arabic with patients. However, in the next three to six months, I became fluent in Arabic. Soon I was able to make diagnoses of several endemic diseases, and I learned how to manage them. From time to time, negative thoughts came to my mind that I was doing more and was overburdened, all while receiving a very low salary. This thinking could bring early frustration, exhaustion, anxiety, or depression and thus lead to burnout. I think all human beings are materialistic and calculate workload with money, and it is true. If I had thought that way, I would have had severe burnout and would be not in this world due to suicide. At this level, I analyzed my personality and my priorities. Did I need to earn money to go back to Pakistan, or would I stay in Saudi Arabia to see how I would survive?

After six months, the medical center director made me chief of medicine without any incentive to increase my salary, but I took that responsibility and successfully managed the department. Within the next year, he made me director of medical services. At this point, my responsibilities were increased, along with patient care and adminis-trative management. Previously, I had not had a chance to work as the director of medical services, dealing with 350 staff members (includ-ing doctors, nurses, and paramedical), conducting several meetings, and playing a decision-making roll in the MOH in Saudi Arabia.

In 1992, the MOH transferred the hospital director to another hospital, and they made me hospital director. My responsibilities increased tenfold, which started unlocking my hidden talents and skill sets. I really enjoyed what I did without any salary increase. I resigned from my job in Saudi Arabia in September 1993 due to the sudden death of my father; I needed to take care of my mother. My final salary was SR 5,600 per month when I left this job.

Now, in the thirty years from 1988 to 2018, I have self-analyzed to learn how I did all that extra hard work with excellence without severe burnout. I reached the final conclusion that we have to set priorities from the beginning that include clarity of mind and maintaining a positive attitude. Life is highly unpredictable, and bad things happen daily, with so many ups and downs. We have to learn to control our emotions to avoid negativity toward life because it will reduce our energy and make our lives dull and boring. Try to maintain positive energy all the time by not discussing any negativity related to others, whether your own family members, friends, or neighbors, because we're all made from the same material—full of weaknesses and with very few strengths. When a negative thought comes, we must learn how to ignore it and forgive everyone right away in order to block the negative thought from continuing in our lives. Life is short. There is no need to compete with others in your life because it will lead to frustration. In this way, you will try to keep your positive energy to focus on the goals you want to achieve for yourself or for your family. Internal happiness is true success.

Today, everyone in life is frustrated, competing with one another and trying to become rich overnight by harming others due to self-ishness. After this job, I became a new person, full of happiness and satisfied with my life. I hope you will also cultivate these abilities to move toward success and mental peace.

After going back to Pakistan in 1993, I got job at Baqai Medical University as an associate professor of medicine. I continued my career successfully. I taught internal and pulmonary medicine to one hundred final-year medical students and fifty dental students. I was providing lectures, bedside teaching, and treatment in wards and clinics. I remember one of my final-year medical students coming to my office because he was struggling in the class. After interacting with him, I noticed that he was under stress, frustrated, and anxious due to obsessing over how he could make money after becoming a doctor and getting a postgraduate degree from the United States or Britain to earn more money like his parents, who were very rich but were suffering from depression and undertreatment. He could not focus due to very high expectations for his future. After a detailed discussion and some relaxation therapy, I provided the real facts of life: that it requires continuous, arduous work with sincerity. There is no harm in earning a lot of money if you plan to earn it honestly. This student was in the expectation and reality phase, and in between was a period of anxiety and stress. I told him that I thought if he could not convert his expectation into reality, then he would be a victim of future burnout, which would spoil his career and personal life. I followed up with this student for three to four months until he understood how to pick the correct pathway to be a confident, honest, and sincere doctor and serve humanity.

I migrated to the United States in 1994 and later worked as a surgical assistant and material management supervisor in 1996 before getting a job in the research and development (R&D) department at the Jesse Brown VA Medical Center (JBVAMC) in October 2000. I worked at the Edgewater Medical Center in Chicago, Illinois. I took care of at least fifteen additional projects with 100 percent outcome and a savings of thousands of dollars. I was promoted to material management supervisor, which further increased my faith in my abilities and my self-confidence with optimal experience, without any additional salary or feelings of burnout.

The hiring person at the JBVAMC interviewed me three times during a three- to four-month period. From my personal evaluation, the hiring person's body language suggested that he was not comfortable offering me the research information specialist position. This was because I did not have any relevant experience working in a R&D department, except for volunteer work at the University of Illinois at Chicago (UIC) in a basic research lab for about three months. The hiring person was right. But I was very confident that I could do the job according to the job requirement as a research information specialist. I reassured the hiring person, but he was reluctant to offer even a part-time job. I was desperate but fully determined that I could do the job well. I suggested giving me a two-week voluntary job in the R&D office to evaluate my work. If the hiring person felt comfortable, then I would have the job; if not, then I would not put in any further requests for the job. The hiring person agreed, and I started work. One cannot imagine what a big challenge it was for me to perform in two weeks to make my career.

There was a high-level research oversight R&D committee meeting the next day. I took charge of the committee meeting arrangements, prepared the meeting agenda, called members about the meeting, and prepared documentation to hold the meeting. This meeting went well, everyone on the committee appreciated my work, and the R&D department boss was happy with me. This encouragement was good enough to get my foot in this department. Over the next two weeks, I took total control and managed several committees and academic affiliates, including the University of Illinois at Chicago Institutional Review Boards (UIC-IRBs) and the Northwestern University Institutional Review Boards (NU-IRBs), as well as various research grants, animal research, and laboratory research. I read all VA policy and procedure handbooks to understand VA research requirements. I was very happy at this achievement. My confidence level and my self-esteem were very high. In the next two months, I got the full-time job. I started my job in the R&D with zero knowledge and nothing but my hard work and a hyperfocus on my daily targets to accomplish work on time. I have worked in this department since then. During the last eighteen years, I have faced a lot of workplace hurdles due to complexity. That is usual everywhere, but it doesn't mean you should be afraid and leave the right career path.

I am a very hard and honest worker, and I give 100 percent effort so that no one can damage me. I never have anxiety or depression or feel unfit for the job, not even in the beginning if there is a mismatch between my skill and the nature of the job, and not even if I am offered additional projects for which I must take full responsibility. If other staff at work refuse to participate as a team, I offer my services to complete the project alone, with 100 percent results and no external reward. My happiness is my love and passion for my daily tasks so that

I can accomplish them to boost my self-confidence and get additional projects. I am always ready to sacrifice my personal time to enhance the organization's reputation.

If you develop this kind of attitude toward work, I assure you there will be no burnout. The organization is a silent observer, but the time will come when management will start appreciating your work and kindness. Even if not, who cares? I am happy with my profession, I love myself, I love with my work, and I love my family. I spend one to two hours with my kids and spouse on a daily basis. It is good enough to keep peace, love, and harmony at home. Your patients, family, and hospital management require a positive attitude, temperament, and passion; this will keep you happy. If you are happy inside, everyone around you looks happy. Try to distribute love among people, and then you will get everything you want in your career—all without frustration and burnout.

Everyone has negative feelings from time to time that can stem from too many job expectations, unchallenging work, a high-pressure environment, low motivation to go to work, frustration, cynicism and negative emotions, or pessimism. Cognitive problems and chronic stress lead to reduced attention and concentration. The body's physiologic mechanism quickly handles these short bursts and returns to normal functioning. This fight-or-flight tunnel vision can negatively affect your ability to solve problems or engage in decision making, and it will increase forgetfulness, which leads to burnout.

The Onset of the Burnout Process According to My Personal Experience

Other new workers do not have these same expectations of themselves for a variety reasons. These workers work only to make ends meet—to earn a living, to provide for their family, or to get the experience they need and move on to the next job. Although none of these motivations are intrinsically wrong, they cannot be the sole reason for why one wakes up in the morning and goes to a nine-to-five job five days a week—that is, if one wants to avoid burnout. Others are also working a second job to meet these latter requirements. At this level, employees feel that it is hard to prioritize tasks according to merit. They start working extra hours and neglect themselves. They jeopardize their own well-being by sacrificing sleep, food, and recreation. Their lifestyle becomes unhealthy. This sensation of being overwhelmed compromises their quality of work as they miss crucial appointments and deadlines in their work settings. This starts with a feeling to do something great for their professional satisfaction and for the success of the organization, but this feeling soon transitions away due to non-cooperation from a coworker or boss. From my personal experience, I noticed that coworkers and those in positions above mine started discouraging me, trying to reduce my enthusiasm, because they were afraid that I would get them demoted or fired for working harder than them. In this way, they started creating hurdles for me. I was assigned additional difficult projects, which augmented stress and frustration. The following example during my first week in Saudi Arabia in the 1980s illustrates this process and how I handled it.

On January 2, 1988, I started my first out-of-country job in Saudi Arabia under the MOH in the Al-Qassim Region as an attending physician and pulmonologist. I came from Pakistan and knew how to speak Urdu and English, but I knew that the patients I would be seeing would primarily be speaking Arabic. I was very motivated to learn the Arabic language as quickly as possible to communicate with my Arabic-speaking patients and provide the best service I could as a doctor. By developing and furthering my language skills in Arabic, I could bolster my patient-doctor relationship, which is at the core of patient care. I could also more prudently and attentively listen to my patients and their health concerns. In doing so, patients would be able to develop trust in me, and I would be able to think of a broad differential diagnosis to successfully manage and treat my patients.

I successfully managed all my patients, regularly following up with them to ensure proper compliance to medications and other

directions of care. Around 10 to 15 percent of my patients needed extra work-ups to obtain the correct diagnosis. This feeling of being able
to work with patients to correctly diagnose their conditions and provide them with a plan of care gave me immense internal satisfaction.
I did not feel burned out because my work was meaningful to me and
gave me pleasure. Once my reputation as a physician increased, more
patients from the province—and even outside the province—came to
our hospital to receive medical care. In this way, I was exposed to more
serious and critical patients, and I was very accepting of the challenge
in managing them. This furthered my clinical intuition and allowed
me to ponder new ways to treat my patients.

I was also very willing to put in extra time for patient management. I never said no because I'd picked this field to treat suffering
people. I had faith in my professional abilities because I had trained
under very rough and tough professors during my clinical rotations
and residency. I also learned from them how I could work confidently
and independently in difficult, high-pressure environments.

Despite having this positive and hardworking mind-set, I soon
came to realize that working in the hospital would not be so simple.
I worked under the hospital director, who had a habit of putting all
his staff in high-pressure situations and trying to micromanage and
control them. He would regularly cut salaries when hospital employees made minor mistakes. For instance, if any hospital staff member
was ten or fifteen minutes late, he would typically cut their salary for
that day if they had come late two or three times prior. He also made
several personal, unannounced rounds in the hospital to check on
his staff, ensuring that they were on task and establishing discipline.
From the very first day I joined this hospital, the other staff members
asked me, "Why did you come to work in this hospital? The hospital
director is a cruel man. It will be hard to work under him."

I responded, "I did not have a choice because the Ministry of
Health selected me for this hospital, and there was a public demand

to have a pulmonologist in this hospital." Their warnings did not have an effect on me. I was determined to do my work as usual.

On the third day of my job, I was on call. All the other attending physicians handed over their critical patients to me. I recall one patient had a complicated medical history. The attending informed me that the patient had diabetic gangrene on his left leg that had spread into his blood, causing septicemia. This was further complicated by his medical history of hypertension, stroke, myocardial infarction, atrial fibrillation, and respiratory failure. That night, I was ready to get a call for this patient because my clinical intuition suggested that something would happen to him. As I predicted, I got a call from the resident at 8:30 p.m. that the patient was in cardiac arrest. I was staying inside the hospital campus at the time and immediately rushed to the hospital to begin my management of the patient. I did my absolute best to stabilize his symptoms, using all my resources to save his life, but unfortunately the patient passed away at 6:00 a.m. I was with the patient the whole night. I prepared the written instructions directed to the nurse and other staff members to hand the body over to the family. I also prepared the death certificate.

At 7:00 a.m., I went home to freshen up because I had to be back at work at 7:30 a.m. for my usual shift. I went to the ward and saw the hospital director, who was looking at the chart for the patient who had passed away earlier that morning. I said good morning to everyone because the other physicians, residents, and nurses were preparing for rounds. The hospital director was also among their company. The hospital director addressed me. "Dr. Salar, I received a complaint against you from the patient's son that you were standing and not doing anything."

I was very frustrated when I heard this and responded, "I did all that I could do as the attending by performing cardiopulmonary resuscitation, injecting lifesaving medications, and providing all other supportive treatment. You can see my progress notes in the file, which I edited every fifteen minutes while managing the patient." I then added, "No attending on-call would ever stay the whole night with a patient under those circumstances. Most would tend to the patient but simply write directions for the resident and nurse to follow. You reviewed the file. If you feel I did not do what needed to be done for this patient, please tell me."

The hospital director blasted me once again. "There was not an issue in managing this dying patient, but there was the complaint."

A part of me could not believe what I was hearing. I felt justified in the way I managed the patient. However, another part of me realized this was the very situation that many of my coworkers had warned me about. I knew his background. It was clear to me that he was trying to control me. As the same time, I was never afraid of having transparency in expressing my thoughts and feelings. I made this quite clear in front of everyone. "Right now, I am resigning from my position and heading back to Pakistan. Please return my passport and arrange my return ticket. I do not want to work under your leadership." I left the place and went to my clinic to see my patients. It was the first time I had felt so angry and frustrated.

For the next six months, I felt burned out. My happy phase of work had come to an end. I despised working under the hospital director, knowing that he would find the minutest of faults in my patient care and management to slander my reputation. I did not feel appreciated at work and lacked a sense of belonging. He would incessantly interfere with my treatment, telling me to give referrals and consults to surgeons and other specialties.

For instance, during this six-month span, I remember one of my patients, a seventeen-year-old farmer, was admitted for breathlessness and chest pain of three days' duration. After performing a physical examination and ordering chest X-rays, I confirmed my clinical suspicion that this patient had a spontaneous pneumothorax, and I decided to pursue conservative treatment without inserting a chest tube directly into his thorax to avoid complications. The hospital director, who was constantly on my back, would read through my patients' notes. He noticed that I decided to not insert a chest tube into this patient and told me to consult with the surgeon to place the chest tube. The surgeon concurred with my conservative treatment, and in the next five days, the patient recovered fully with this type of care. This was one of the first incidences during which I was able to develop confidence in my abilities. I was able to make my own decisions and control my destiny. Despite what the hospital director, my boss, had said, my treatment proved to be absolutely correct; a more invasive treatment would be have been contingent to more complications and may have worsened the patient's already poor condition.

There were several examples of when I felt that I had triumphed and overcome any potential flaws or weaknesses in my abilities during this period. This feeling helped me combat the burnout I felt when I first started working at the hospital. For example, a seventy-year-old male patient presented to the ER with a twelve-hour history of stroke and a prior history of hypertension and diabetes. On examination, this patient had right-sided hemiparesis, in which the right half of his body was paralyzed. I promptly prepared a request for a brain CT scan to determine whether the patient had an ischemic or hemorrhagic stroke. At this time, both the medical center director and the hospital director called me into their office. They asked, "Dr. Salar, why do you need a CT scan when you can manage conservatively?"

I asked them, "You are both medical doctors and are telling me that a patient, who may have a stroke based on his presentation, does not need a CT scan and should be treated conservatively? Because treatment of an ischemic stroke is much different from a hemorrhagic stroke, I am going to have to obtain the CT scan and start my treatment accordingly." They were clearly upset. Because our hospital facility lacked a CT machine, I needed to send the patient to another nearby hospital with the technology to get this imaging completed. However, they both vehemently refused to sign the referral. Without thinking, I grabbed the referral from their side of the table and told them, "Because you both are refusing to sign this referral, I will make a note on it that you two will be liable for this patient's well-being if he experiences future complications due to negligence." I had unintentionally created a scene. They were both livid but acquiesced to my demands. They half-heartedly signed the referral.

The patient went for the CT scan, and the results came back the same day as positive for a thrombus as the cause of his ischemic stroke. I started anticoagulation therapy with other supportive treatment for the patient. Fortunately, this patient recovered 90 percent of his original functionality with rehabilitation over the next six months. I regularly followed up with this patient every month in my clinic. Because the patient's home was five hundred kilometers away, I recommended this patient's family to maintain a follow-up hospital within close proximity to their house. However, they refused to go to any hospital because they trusted me with his health. The patient's son told me, "If you did not take the step to treat my father, he would not be in good health today. We would be happy to drive five hundred kilometers to come for the monthly follow-up." I felt this was the best way to stand for a worthy cause. I did not let the potential fear of losing my job overcome me. I had faith in my abilities and was not afraid to take a stand against my hospital management administrators. After this incident, they were even more upset with me, and they intently kept their eyes on me and my patient care to catch any error to justify my firing. Despite this looming in the background, I strived for what I believed was excellence in patient care.

One can imagine that working on a daily basis under these kinds of stressful situations was not an easy task. The first six months were extremely harsh for me from the hospital director, and I quite naturally developed feelings of tension, frustration, hopelessness, negativity, worthlessness, and prolonged stress. I felt that I was already at the halfway point of being completely burned out. I would see the hospital director secretly observe me every day, trying to provoke me into making mistakes. The nonverbal message he was trying to get across was that he would not leave me alone. Every week, he would call me into his office two to three times for some minor issues to put me under pressure. So far, he could not find any mistake great enough to punish me. That was indeed a period of trial and tribulation for me. Due to my personal experience working as a psychiatrist in a psychiatry hospital in Pakistan prior to coming to Saudi Arabia, I knew my personality. I knew how to combat chronic stress situations and avoid any compromising of my career, health, and well-being in the future. I started to tackle my tumultuous situation by practicing self-control, maintaining self-confidence, and having faith in my abilities. I tried to focus on the current target so as to not dwell on the past or become hyperfocused about the future. I ultimately took this situation upon myself as a personal challenge—to show that I was indeed competent in my profession and to let people around me know that I am strong and fully determined to accomplish my career goals.

During this entire six-month period, I reassured myself that I was indeed competent enough to control my workplace tension, pressures, stresses, frustrations, anxiety, and the feeling of being overwhelmed. I continued to push through by keeping alive my intrinsic motivation behind working as a physician, having compassion and an enthusiastic approach toward patients. I had taken an interest in Arabic and took the time to learn it to connect with my patients, and my hard work seemed to have paid off because many of my patients were happy with my management of their conditions.

Despite feeling burned out during this time, I was able to self-reflect, put my feelings aside, and focus on my goals as a physician: to provide the best care to my patients. I was able to unlock and identify my hidden talents and skill sets to tackle this difficult situation with the utmost degree of confidence and clarity of mind. By doing this, I was able to overcome many of these negative feelings, which provided me with a sense of internal happiness and satisfaction. The point I am trying to get across is that if you start experiencing these symptoms, then you should not become complacent. You should try to identify the cause of the burnout in your particular situation and strive to change your situation to resolve it. If it continues, burnout can lead to chronic stress and manifest itself as severe burnout. Burnout can then also lead to depression and diminished job performance. Workplace burnout is now becoming a worldwide epidemic and is composed of physical and emotional exhaustion, depersonalization, and low personal achievements.

At the end of April or May 1988, I was in the ER when I got a call from my director that the director at Buraidah Mental Health Hospital had requested to talk to me. The hospital director asked him, "Do you have a complaint against Dr. Salar? Please tell me."

The psychiatry hospital director told him, "I want to acknowledge and appreciate Dr. Salar's expertise in the field of psychiatry. I want to speak with him." He was pleased and happy with my accurate and detailed diagnoses, as well as my treatment plans related to the referral of psychiatry patients. Their hospital's psychiatrists were not doing much workup with patient examination. He requested that I not provide any psychiatric or mental evaluation of the patients that I would refer out to his psychiatry hospital. I was informed to simply write my name and diagnosis on the referral so that the psychiatrists trained in their positions could do the appropriate workup. I came to realize that such praise did not come overnight.

After this incident, I gradually started to notice a stark and peculiar change in the hospital's director's demeanor toward me. After one month, in June or July 1988, a miracle happened. The hospital director called me into his office and said, "I have decided to make you chief of medicine."

I was completely shocked. It illustrated to me that by engaging in positive thinking and staying focused on my goals and aspirations despite the difficulties that life sent my way during this span, I was able to succeed and come out on top. At the same time, I took this opportunity with a grain of salt because I figured he would put me under more stress if I became his chief of medicine. Right away, I refused his offer. "You already created enough trouble for me. I am rejecting your offer."

He said, "You will not leave my office unless you change your mind and accept this position." In an act of rebellion, I sat on the sofa in his office, directly facing him. He would perform his work and would intermittently ask, "Have you changed your mind?" I replied no every time. He said, "I will not let you leave the office until you say yes." I sat in the room the whole day. At the end of day, he told me, "You will report back to my room tomorrow, and remember that this will continue until you accept my offer."

At this point, I had to ask him, "Why are you insisting? The current chief is a very good and respected doctor. I will work more closely with him to help him in his administrative duties."

He said, "Dr. Salar, I was behind you for the last six months to test your patient care and decision making. Your cure rate was superb. No other physician will match your expertise, even in diagnosing psychiatric illnesses. I got a call from the director at the nearby psychiatric hospital who commented that your diagnosis is even better than the psychiatrists working in the hospital. This is the reason I want you to be chief of medicine." This was the best compliment I could have received. At that moment, I could not do anything but accept his offer. He issued the order that very same day, and I started my position as the chief of medicine.

Chapter 6

The Phases of the Burnout Process

In the process of burnout, various signs and symptoms are manifested. These are very different in the beginning and end phases, but at the same time they are intimately related to one another and run on a spectrum. These symptoms can manifest as anxiety or depression, as well as a multitude of other conditions. Nonetheless, these signs and symptoms are interconnected, and by correctly identifying the phase that you are in, you can then take steps to resolve them.

Burnout is linked to a series of interconnected events of signs and symptoms, such as apprehension, tension, and pressure, and they progress on a spectrum and inevitably get worse in time. These symptoms may eventually advance depression, suicidal ideation, and ultimately suicide. Regardless of where you work, whether in an occupational, business, educational, or health-care profession, the term *burnout* is universal. It is unequivocally used to describe the feelings of weariness and fatigue that overcome those affected by it. I hope this chapter will convey a level of clarity about the step-by-step process of burnout and, in doing so, put you on the correct path to self-manage it—or in extreme situations, to seek advice from a psychologist or psychiatrist.

According to psychologists Herbert Freudenberger and Gail North, burnout has twelve phases, and there is no clear line of demarcation from one phase to another.[15] Therefore their work echoes the fact that burnout is on a continuum. The burnout process will not necessarily have a clear transition from one phase to another, and thus the progression thereof will ultimately differ from one burnout victim to another.

In my personal experience and observation, the onset of burnout is not simple. It is a complicated process consisting of your thought process and personality. What is your perception of your working environment? How do you respond to changes in your work environment? What role does your personality play in this? The answer to these questions is variable, but it plays a pivotal role in identifying how your progression of burnout will differ from another's. You may go through all the phases I describe next or perhaps only a few, with no clear handover to the next phase. Based on my thirty-seven years of job experience and observations, I have identified eighteen phases of burnout.

Burnout Phase 1: The Happy Phase of Work

When starting a new job with confidence and motivation, I call this the happy phase of work. You are excited to begin a new journey in your life. Whether this is your very first job or your seventeenth, you look forward to what awaits you in your new work environment. Because you were selected for this position, presumably through some form of assessment and interview criteria, you feel that you have the prerequisites to do the job well. Initially, you strive for success, performing tasks well or even beyond your job description, to please the higher-ups and to demonstrate a degree of competency.

You have high self-esteem, ambition, motivation, enthusiasm, passion, and a full determination to leave your mark on your employment and employer. In order to be considered as equals to your peers, you

---

[15] Herbert J. Freudenberger and Gail North, *Women's Burnout: How to Spot It, How to Reverse It, and How to Prevent It* (New York: Doubleday, 1985).

must work at least as hard as they do. This also accelerates your standing in the organization. At the very least, you want to be considered as equal to your coworkers and to be given the corresponding regard and respect you deserve for your work.

You may start working harder to meet your personal high expectations, going beyond the job description. You accept more work and finish tasks prior to deadlines. I have felt the same at the beginning of each new job in my time in Pakistan, Saudi Arabia, and America. I owe this mentality to how I was raised during my childhood. My parents trained me starting at twelve years of age by giving me the autonomy to make decisions. They gave me the freedom to cook, clean, and even do interior design in my spare time. In this way, I acquired basic organizational skills, time management, and reverence and respect for my elders. This kind of work fueled my personal goals and ambitions in life and furthered me as a person, giving me a sense of satisfaction and internal happiness. I found this additional work meaningful. This mind-set allowed me to accept any task or challenge because it provided me with a sense of pleasure.

Solution to Prevent Phase 1 of Burnout

The reason for my success is not having any expectation to increase my salary or receive awards and recognition. I was able to develop my internal feelings of happiness after successful completion of daily tasks, which maintains my energy and intrinsic motivation to perform well all the time. In this way, I avoided the onset of the burnout process. I believe that anyone working only for external monitoring awards will be more prone to burnout because expectation outstrips reality, which can be heartbreaking and lead to frustration and negativity. If you will follow in my footsteps, I assure you that it will prevent the onset of burnout from the very beginning.

Burnout Phase 2: Overwork

The reason for overworking is that you are expecting too much from your supervisor in terms of awards or salary increase. Some professionals become fully devoted to work without their will; in other words it may be a mismatch between work and their real desires. If you do anything without passion and interest, then you will lose the determination and energy to accomplish job projects and will move to the exhaustion phase of burnout.

Solution to Prevent Phase 2 of Burnout

I was assigned additional difficult projects at work, which augmented my stress and frustration. This eventually led to feeling overworked, which is a feeling of tiredness or decreased energy due to a gradual decrease in passion for your work that is not reciprocated with internal or external rewards. Try to keep your expectations at low levels if you think your supervisor will give you a raise so that you don't become frustrated and exhausted when that does not happen, which will break your heart and start eroding your mind. Keep a healthy balance between work and life. Spend time daily with friends outside your job to release your emotions by not talking about workplace issues, which will make you more frustrated. Daily walks or watching television keep me relaxed and stress-free.

Burnout Phase 3: Exhaustion

This phase begins with fatigue that can become chronic if your negative thinking persists. Fatigue occurs due to a loss of the passion and motivation you first had for your work when you started your job. You now feel inexplicably tired and have low energy levels. These symptoms can induce sleep disturbances and interfere with other aspects of your life. You start to feel overwhelmed, even with the smallest of tasks at home or at work. If you notice these changes early and try to adopt preventive measures to counteract these feelings, then it is possible to avoid the more severe stages of burnout.

In the beginning, you try to fit into the organization and to meet its high expectations. You have a strong will and an intrinsic motivation to succeed, but if your expectations don't meet reality, then this positive mind-set can lead to a negative mind-set and approach. If you do not have intrinsic motivation, you won't take on additional work and will even struggle with daily work because you have lost interest, which leads to frustration and anxiety. If you are in this position, stop doing extra work. If it is not being asked of you extrinsically and it does not bring you any intrinsic pleasure, then you should make the conscientious decision to move forward with change. Doing extra will only exacerbate the burnout. If leaving your current workplace is not a viable option, then focus on your job according to its requirements to prevent further burnout.

Solution to Prevent Phase 3 of Burnout

Seek advice from your supervisor and coworkers to determine whether the work at hand matches your skill set or whether you need a little extra help to complete your work-related tasks. Burnout is manageable at this level. You need to find it within you to avoid complacency, find the root source of the issue, and target it at that level. If you do not control it at this point, then you will move to the next phase of burnout.

Burnout Phase 4: Deterioration of Focus on Work

Failure to focus on daily tasks and being unable to perform daily activities that result in missing deadlines leads to the beginning of stress and a loss of confidence in your ability to perform a job.

Solution to Prevent Phase 4 of Burnout

Work overload leads to tension and pressure, as well as feelings of being overwhelmed, which enhances forgetfulness. It also reduces your attention and concentration at work. To improve your focus on your job, you must reorganize your daily tasks and split them into smaller, more achievable tasks. Then think how you can work to get results. If you feel you need some expert help, ask your supervisor to provide guidance in understanding the nature of your work. You have to take this task as a challenge to get positive results within a designated time frame to meet your supervisor's expectations. After achieving a positive outcome, you will gain self-confidence and clarity of mind to perform your work according to its merit, which will build your attention and concentration. It will increase your focus on getting results. After this, you can start feeling happy in your heart, which will give your strong feelings of energy.

Burnout Phase 5: Beginning of Physical Complaints

At this stage, you develop more physical symptoms, such as muscle pain, back pain, gastrointestinal symptoms, and a lowered immune system, which leads to frequent cold symptoms. Remember to be honest in your self-analysis to determine the source of the problem and how you can rectify the issues to move on with confidence. If you do not find the needed solutions, then physical symptoms start, which is the beginning of burnout in the near future.

Solution to Prevent Phase 5 of Burnout

The best way to deal with this phase is by using your positive energy through positive thinking. These are all symptoms of psychosomatic illness and they cause you to feel negatively toward your workplace and your personal life. You can covert negativity by using your positive thinking. For example, think that lot of people do not have jobs, but you have a job. You prepare daily to go to work. On the road each day, hundreds and thousands of people go to work to provide food and shelter for their families. Get positive energy from this crowd. Try to work hard with your sincerity to become more interested in your job.

Burnout Phase 6: Anxiousness

You are anxious and fearful over losing your job due to failure of job performance.

Solution to Prevent Phase 6 of Burnout

Any kind of fear reduces your confidence and increases your anxiety, sometimes in the form of a panic attack. If these continue, acute stress can lead to persistent chronic stress. Start by managing your stress to relax and reduce your anxiety, which will rebuild your confidence in your own abilities. People know their own ways of relaxing and coping with stress. I am fully relaxed by watching political commentary on television for one hour daily. After this, I get back my energy to return to my daily tasks and internal happiness.

Burnout Phase 7: Physical and Mental Fatigue

If you exhaust all your energy, then you become irritable. At this stage, you do not know how to achieve physical and mental relaxation. Thus, you become emotionally blunted when in social gatherings or at home with family. You look sad, are obsessed, are self-occupied, and suffer from an internal fear of losing your job due to failure to accomplish job assignments on time. If this is not controlled or treated, it will lead to personality damage and reduce attraction to life and family.

Solution to Prevent Phase 7 of Burnout

This phase of burnout requires immediate consultation with a primary care physician, psychologist, or psychiatrist in order to receive treatment and stop the progression to depression.

Burnout Phase 8: Insomnia

Due to chronic stress and anxiety, you start experiencing poor sleep, which exacerbates current feelings of fatigue and exhaustion and increases irritability.

Solution to Prevent Phase 8 of Burnout

This phase of burnout requires immediate consultation with a primary care physician, psychologist, or psychiatrist in order receive treatment and stop the progression to depression.

Burnout Phase 9: Onset of Anger

Anger will develop because you are unable to do things and to accomplish your daily goals.

Solution to Prevent Phase 9 of Burnout

Start with relaxation therapy to reduce anger. Split your daily tasks into smaller units so that you can accomplish tasks on time while building your confidence. Assure yourself that you still have the potential to manage daily tasks.

Burnout Phase 10: Aggression and Irritability

Socially isolating yourself due to your intolerance of people can cause you to feel aggression and become more sarcastic.

Solution to Prevent Phase 10 of Burnout

This phase of burnout requires immediate consultation with a primary care physician, psychologist, or psychiatrist in order to receive treatment and stop the progression to depression.

Burnout Phase 11: Beginning of Isolation (Social Withdrawal)

You feel rejected, so you isolate yourself and avoid social gatherings.
Solution to Prevent Phase 11 of Burnout

This phase of burnout requires immediate consultation with a primary care physician, psychologist, or psychiatrist in order to receive treatment and stop the progression to depression.

Burnout Phase 12: Onset of Drug and Alcohol Addiction

Due to the beginnings of depression, you have developed feelings of hopelessness and helplessness, which lead you to become involved with drugs and alcohol.

Solution to Prevent Phase 12 of Burnout

This phase of burnout requires immediate consultation with a primary care physician, psychologist, or psychiatrist in order to receive treatment and stop the progression to depression.

Burnout Phase 13: Changing in Body Language and Behavior

These changes in body language and behavior are noticeable and alarming to others.

Solution to Prevent Phase 13 of Burnout

This phase of burnout requires immediate consultation with a primary care physician, psychologist or psychiatrist in order to receive treatment and stop the progression to depression.

Burnout Phase 14: Feelings of Worthlessness

You develop feelings of worthlessness and believe that you do not provide value to the community. You become more mechanical, without human feelings.

Solution to Prevent Phase 14 of Burnout

This phase of burnout requires immediate consultation with a primary care physician, psychologist or psychiatrist in order to receive treatment and stop the progression to depression.

Burnout Phase 15: Empty Feeling

You begin feeling empty inside. To overcome this empty feeling, you may engage in overeating or frequent sex.

Solution to Prevent Phase 15 of Burnout

This phase of burnout requires immediate consultation with a primary care physician, psychologist or psychiatrist in order to receive treatment and stop the progression to depression.

Burnout Phase 16: Emotional Detachment

You start arriving late for work and disconnecting from family and friends, signaling the start of emotional and environmental detachment.

Solution to Prevent Phase 16 of Burnout

This phase of burnout requires immediate consultation with a primary care physician, psychologist or psychiatrist in order to receive treatment and stop the progression to depression.

Burnout Phase 17: Depression

This is a serious phase and may lead to suicide. You no longer experience enjoyment in life, no longer feel that you provide value to society, and start to believe that life has no meaning. You are exhausted and feel hopeless, helpless, cynical, resentful, and indifferent. You have nothing more to give and are now entering into depression. If it continues, suicidal thoughts will come again and again due to your feelings of worthlessness, and you may turn to suicide.

Solution to Prevent Phase 17 of Burnout

This phase of burnout requires immediate consultation with a primary care physician, psychiatrist for admission to the hospital to begin treatment with antidepressants and prevent suicide.

Burnout Phase 18: Final Burnout Phase

During the entirety of the depression phase, you will have imploded physically and emotionally and will need immediate medical treatment in the hospital due to feelings of hopelessness. You feel that you are sitting in a dark tunnel and have no hope. Hopelessness is the symptom of depression that leads to burnout.

Solution to Prevent Phase 18 of Burnout

This phase of burnout requires immediate consultation with a psychiatrist for admission to the hospital to begin treatment with antidepressants and prevent suicide.

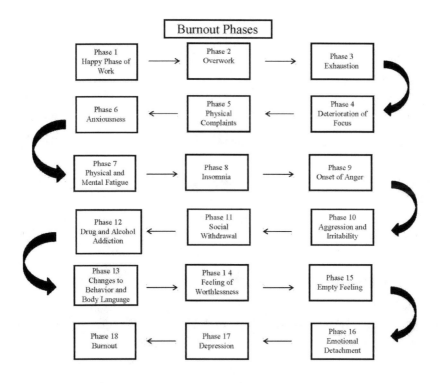

Chapter 7

Step-by-Step Self-Care
Solution of Burnout

1. Screening and Counseling

If you are a physician suffering from burnout, as I did, write down your medical and family history, socioeconomic level, and drug and alcohol use, and present and past occupational environment to find an immediate cause of your burnout. Think about your various fears that may be due to negative thinking patterns, lack of motivation for your chosen career, poor work environment, and poor spousal relations. The ability to honestly self-evaluate your own mental status will help you find the signs of early burnout. After extensive intervention, the cause of burnout is often found and will help you to manage early burnout easily. In this way, we can stop the development of deadly burnout in the future and possibly eliminate it for good.

A good history-taking of illness and a clinical examination is important to rule out underlying causes of burnout. You may need to consult other physicians with knowledge of a burnout victim's clinical presentation to help you or anyone who is feeling that something abnormal going on in their minds relating to workplace needs. You can also consult a family physician for evaluation of early burnout.

If endocrinological conditions (hormone-related illnesses) such as hyperthyroidism or pituitary adenoma are the underlying cause of anxiety and depression, then we must treat the cause. In my clinical practice, I diagnosed several patients with pituitary gland adenoma (tumor of one of the hormone centers of the brain) that was being treated as depression by a psychiatrist. Determining the underlying causes of stress is important; if physiologic reasons are ruled out, then we can start with a mental status examination to rule out any psychological illness or work-related stress.

The self-management plan for burnout will start at each level of early onset of symptoms to achieve satisfactory results.

To overcome a reduction in personal accomplishments, start by making some adjustments in your daily work environment, such as setting smaller daily targets in order to control work tasks and achieve a positive outcome, develop self-motivation and feelings of self-reward for doing a decent job, and appreciate team members for their support. Let's examine the idea of setting smaller targets; their power is exemplified here. In my case, I have multiple tasks and deadlines. For example, a noncompliance report has many moving parts. I need to have a specific plan in my mind and to understand the nature of the project. This involves what I need from others and what I need to do myself. This often means having meetings and requesting data from researchers. Sometimes it can be difficult to get hold of them. Once a meeting is established and we convene, we discuss the noncompliance and identify the problem. Once discussed, I create training to rectify the mistake and develop a report that is forwarded to the appropriate internal committees. They present their recommendations, and I finalize my report for research oversight. Afterward, I prepare for submission and discussion with the director and chief of staff. The report is then forwarded to the Office of Research Oversight, and at our facility, we discuss how we can rectify and make changes to the research program to improve service to our veterans. As you can see, this is a very dynamic project, and it is only one of many projects I handle. Challenges include technical and communication aspects. However, by breaking down this process and focusing on one component at a time, I make the task more manageable, and every success in these smaller goals can be used as stepping stones on my path to achievement.

There is also an exhilaration in solving these challenges and seeing what you are capable of. This is the concept of eustress and its benefits. Students are under a lot of stress to maintain good grades, meet professional and personal challenges, keep up their self-motivation, and remain hyperfocused to achieve optimal experiences that add to their skill sets and ultimately provide them with self-confidence. All these enjoyments require positive thinking.

As a burnout victim, ideally you could follow up with a family physician who can screen and identify burnout. However, currently there is no screening tool. I have attempted to create one for family physicians. In my opinion, there are many in society who have undiagnosed burnout that could lead to negative outcomes for society in terms of productivity. More frequent psychological evaluations can prevent burnout. There must be no stigma associated with these kinds of evaluations. There must be more training of psychiatrists and psychologists in order to evaluate everyone once in their lifetimes regarding their personality types, behaviors, and attitudes. If negative thought patterns are identified, then positive thinking or proper treatment can be prescribed. It can lead to success in the workplace and in family life. Problems in personality, behavior, and attitude that are successfully resolved with this method can lead to improvement at the societal level.

You must be open and ask for help to seek the best advice and moral support. Try to learn how to manage stress. Discuss specific concerns with an appropriate colleague, supervisor, or manager to find the best solutions to such issues, such as flexible work hours or using a mentor to improve the skills you need to perform your work. If there is an attitude issue, then you must correct it. You must find ways to stay relaxed and happy to improve performance. Try to control unreasonable and unrealistic demands. Learn how to avoid work-related stress.

Maybe even look for another job that suits your happiness. Learn to balance or control negative feelings to move more toward a positive attitude, which will protect you from emotional exhaustion. Further interventions will depend on your needs and may include relaxation techniques, counseling, or psychotherapy.

2. Work and Life Balance

Burnout is common in any workplace environment. It begins with overwhelming situations—your mind obsesses about work, which reduces your efficacy and shakes your confidence. According to my experience and observation, I divided the process of burnout into various steps to ease understanding of a management plan according to your level of burnout.

Step 1: Feeling Overwhelmed (First Negative Feelings)

The first burnout symptom starts with feeling almost as if you are drowning. These negative effects of burnout influence every aspect of life, including your home, work, and social life. In fact, people have told me at work that "every day is a bad day," or they ask, "What is new in a day?" It appears that caring about work or home life is a waste of energy. It means to me that the people are exhausted and moving toward burnout; they are losing control at work and feeling overwhelmed. It means they have a poor capacity to perform a job with a high workload, and they have no control to complete the task on time due to a lack of motivation, uncooperative coworkers, unfair treatment, or conflicting values. How can you manage this feeling of being overwhelmed?

You can start by thinking about a workable solution to block this negative feeling with a positive outcome. If someone says that she hates this job or that type of work, then it means to me that the person is a negative thinker. I never use negative words, even though I have failed so many times. Instead, I use the power of positive criticism to try to correct myself and to never blame others. If you learn to see the world without wearing dark glasses, understand other human beings, forgive their mistakes, and correct your own mistakes, then you will be on the right pathway to happiness.

If you have started a new job or even your first job, you may not have enough experience or skills to tackle the requirements. Start by using your mind to figure out how you can confidently perform your duties by setting smaller daily targets. This will reduce your workload and allow you to avoid feeling overwhelmed. It is a continuous process, and gradually your body and mind will be trained to accept more and more work if you are realistic and happy to take on additional responsibilities. After this, you will be used to these types of work environments and will start enjoying your work. Even as you strive to minimize this feeling of being overwhelmed, it means you have to dig deep within yourself to identify the mismatch between your experience and skill. If this gap is too much, you will not survive in the future with this job, even if you have some motivation and feel that you can manage, unless you have strong determination and the self-confidence to learn fast to overcome these weaknesses. You can use your strong positive feelings to work toward success, which is inspired by keeping the idea alive in your mind that you are a fighter, that you know the company is good and you have a bright future ahead, that the salary and benefits are good, and most important that the work environment is supportive so that you will gain more experience and skill to compensate for any weaknesses. These factors will give you control over your overwhelming feelings and turn them into a positive attitude. If you cannot do it, you can look for new job where your experience will match your skills. These actions will keep you from future burnout.

Step 2: Simple Stress (Feelings of Pressure or Tension)

If overwhelming feelings continue, it will take you to the next level of subjective feelings of pressure or tension with some obsession (repeated thought of work overload), which leads to stress. If job pressures and tensions are not managed properly and you cannot find a better solution to fight against these factors, it will lead to a change in the personal psyche. This is the early phase of simple stress. Everyone feels pressure and tension related to a consequence of one's daily routine life, which usually passes away easily without harming anyone. But if it is persistent, then it can have consequences on one's life and health. Some stress is situational and goes away by itself in time. If it is self-imposed (due to the presence of an anxious personality), then it may require consultation with a psychologist. For me, these factors belong to negative thinking patterns that must be changed to a positive attitude toward work and life. How can you release the pressure or tension of work?

The human body has a great physiologic adaptation mechanism to keep you from a state of obsession, tension, or pressure by diverting your attention toward other positive elements of the job and asking for help or guidance from your coworkers or even from your boss. Gain positive energy by relaxing during the workday for a few minutes from time to time if you have done something good. You will be reassured that you have the capabilities and abilities to perform well under stress. Please do not forget to appreciate yourself on a daily basis, even for very minor accomplishments. I assure you it will build your self-confidence and maintain some level of self-motivation to continue in your work, which will gradually improve your job performance. Remember that everyone needs a job to survive in this world. Everyone must do something to survive. You will also need to do something for your future. Please do not give space in your mind that can develop a fear of failure; this is a major killer of your self-confidence and bright future. If you succeed in developing self-confidence, clarity of vision, and self-analysis skills, and if you do not give in to a fear of failure, I assure you that you will be the strongest person on earth. Do not worry; you have plenty of time to get a grip on the situation.

Step 3: Chronic Stress (Psychological)

This is the decisive step that leads to future burnout. If simple stress continues beyond your control, it will transform into a chronic, persistent feeling of stress and result in several psychological symptoms that affect personal health. Burnout is multifactorial in nature. One of the major causes of burnout is chronic stressors. These continue for a long time on a daily basis when you cannot find ways to resolve the issue. Everyone handles stress in different ways. You can tackle stress alone by making certain changes in your daily life. Start thinking that stress is a part of life. Teach your body how to cope with it. Through this, you will find a path to daily relaxation. Chronic stress is characterized by the following feelings, as described by burnout victims.

+ Mental exhaustion and low energy
+ Decreased levels of enthusiasm and motivation
+ Feelings of ineffectiveness
+ Frustration, cynicism, or pessimism; this negative thinking leads to poor health

A psychologist must evaluate any phase of chronic stress. This will inform you how to control burnout at this stage to avoid further progression into feelings of worthlessness, depersonalization, detachment, depression, and suicide.

At this phase, you must create a balance between work and life by making changes in your daily schedule. You must find time to relax—to keep work and life together—because both are essential for your survival. How do you relax? What is meaningful to you?

You must find different ways to relax depending on your personality. Some options to consider are getting a good night's sleep, eating healthy food, watching movies, playing sports, shopping, listening to music, spending time with like-minded people, or reading a book.

In my case, I feel fully relaxed after watching political talk shows on current affairs for one to two hours or by listening to music. These activities reduce my stress level and relax my body and mind. Doing these things has helped me to relax and be strongly self-motivated to complete my eight-hour shift in four to six hours with a high level of brain alertness and a clear vision about what to do and how to do it with high standards, a real feeling of satisfaction, and internal happiness on completion of the task. I quickly achieved this goal by practicing and by gradually reducing my task completion time period. Remember, practice makes you perfect. I still use this technique when I travel from home to work each day. If you hold a high-level position and have many projects that require you to multitask, you need un-interrupted focus to complete your projects, perhaps even one to two weeks before the deadline. To do this without becoming frustrated or overwhelmed, you need to keep alive your high motivation and high energy by relaxing on a daily basis, spending time with family, playing with your children, or doing charity work to benefit others. Remember, there are a fair share of poor and needy people who have been left behind due to the failure of our system and society to bring them back to flow with other successful people through good edu-cation and job training. There was a great contribution from several people, including my parents, to help me attain the position I have today.

Work-related stress is a natural phenomenon. My routine is the same every morning. I travel nearly one hour to work. Once in the office, I'm ready for a marathon of several questionable e-mails, issues, incidences, and noncompliance issues. I prepare for meetings and read meeting materials so that I can participate. This is very interesting and gives me a sense of my value to the organization. It is only possible due to my sincerity to my job and my desire to learn from others ev-ery day. In addition, I do many things that are not related to my job, but if my boss asks me to resolve an issue to enhance the process of completing a task, I accept this as a challenge to get another chance to go into a state of flow, where I can enjoy an optimum experience and receive internal happiness. This refreshes me and produces new energy within me so that I can start another new project. For me, life is about doing challenging work with positive results. I feel the pleasure of satisfaction upon completing these challenges, which doubles my energy. Teach your body and mind how you can make yourself the happiest person on earth. For me, additional money has no value. I feel comfortable whatever I am earning from my regular job. I never put my life in jeopardy to make myself a money-making machine. I learn how I can feel happy with limited resources and adjust my happiness around it. However, this does not mean that I will not look for opportunities for a better salary. I have set my priorities in regard to how much I need for my family. I will never make a decision to earn five to ten thousand dollars extra out of state. I always keep my family with me because I am a family-oriented man. You may think that I am crazy and do not belong to this world. It is not true. My priority is to keep my self-motivation alive, to learn or do something new to keep attraction in my life. This is my life and my happiness with my greatest relaxation. I do not need to go on vacation or spend time with friends unnecessarily. I spend time experimenting with and preparing various types of foods as well as changing house decorations and settings at least four or five times a year. I change wall colors and buy new decorative pieces or good pictures related to natural beauty. All this relaxes me. I spend more time at home and cleaning my house, which gives me more happiness than anything else. I have been practicing these things for the last fifty years, since the age of twelve. Now, I am glad that my wife and two sons follow my legacy.

Chronic Stress Leads to Burnout

Step 1: Feeling Overwhelmed (Negative Feelings)

↓

Step 2: Simple Stress (Feelings of Pressure and Tension)

↓

Step 3: Chronic Stress (Psychological)

3. Self-Care Guide to the Early Phases of Burnout

The first negative feeling starts a chain reaction that leads to burnout, as follows.

Overwhelmed à Simple Stress à Chronic Stress
à Frustration à Exhaustion à Irritability

If this process continues, it will begin to erode your mental capacity, and it will advance the onset of burnout.

The first step in identifying early burnout is to recognize which stage you are in, as outlined earlier. Are you overwhelmed? Are you experiencing simple stress on a daily basis? Are you at the point of experiencing chronic stress? Are you frustrated? Are you mentally exhausted? Are you irritable?

After identifying the stage, you are in, you can think of solutions to control the progression of burnout as soon as possible. You must recognize the root cause of these symptoms, whether it's due to high work demand or the time frame required to accomplish a work task. What does your superior expect of you? What are your expectations? By answering these questions, you can take the first step toward addressing the situation. You may need to consult your boss, supervisor, coworkers, or even someone outside your work environment to provide guidance.

Be honest with yourself in finding the solution to your job-related issues so that you can overcome your overwhelming situation. Remember that there is a solution for every issue or problem. Always think positively and act confidently. Always be ready to learn from anyone, whether from a junior coworker or from your kids, spouse, family, and friends. I implement this philosophy on a daily basis. I am never hesitant to learn from anyone, and I correct myself daily. All human beings are born with several weaknesses and very few strengths. It means no one is perfect, but if you start overcoming your weaknesses, you will boost your self-confidence. Later, you will learn that you can convert your weaknesses into strengths. Always try to reassure yourself—you can do it, nothing is impossible—and your sincere efforts will lead to confidence and will build your future as a strong person with the ability to do anything you'd like. The key to your success is insightfulness related to your job. You need some background knowledge and ability to perform your work. It is my observation that no two working environments are alike, even if the nature of the work is similar. The work environment depends on the boss. If the boss lacks confidence and is prone to panic, aggression, inflexibility, and confusion; if the boss is unaware of workers' experience and skill levels; and if the boss does not successfully communicate the ins and outs of work projects, then worker expectations will be unclear, and this will create chaos in the department. That is when the blame game starts.

Knowledge of how to carry out a project according to its merit will build your self-confidence, clarify your goals, and uncloud your vision once you implement the process to accomplish a goal with positive outcomes. It will build faith in your long-term abilities, and nobody will beat your job performance; even if you go anywhere in the world, you will be the most successful in the worst work environment with the worst boss. If your coworkers are reluctant to work as a team on additional projects, you will have the faith and self-confidence in your own abilities do it alone. Please try to develop your own style to work independently with immense success and become a role model for others who may fear failure. Believe me, nobody will beat your arduous work ethic, honesty, and sincerity when you are ready to sacrifice your time and money for the organization or for humanity. Once you are able to apply all these factors, you will move toward perfection.

Remember, you must tell the truth at the time of the job interview about your skills and experience. I have observed that if a job does not match your skills and experience, you will invite trouble from the very beginning. The only thing that may lead to your survival is hard work, showing an eagerness to learn fast with intrinsic motivation, and asking questions if there is any difficulty facing you at work.

4. Maintain Low to Moderate Expectations
to Avoid the Onset of Burnout

Here I outline various solutions to self-manage burnout by maintaining low to moderate expectations.

Consider this: A future burnout victim starts a job with high expectations and an enthusiastic approach, but sooner or later the person begins losing control due to workplace negativity and moves toward feelings of inefficiency. You are the person having issues, and you need to honestly self-analyze the work environment to find the mismatch between your job and your skills and to determine how fast you can learn the new job and develop the ability to perform the work according to the job requirements. The amount of time you will need to reassure yourself that you will gain control of your job duties is three to six months, or perhaps even more.

Always ask questions and try to learn how to avoid future burnout. In the beginning, you are very passionate about your job but then gradually lose that passion. Why? This may be due to a negative work environment. Perhaps the boss and other staff feel insecure due to your high energy, passion, skill, and experience, and they create hurdles for you or give you a difficult time so that you, an enthusiastic person, will quit your job.

According to my experience and observation while treating thousands of patients in my medical practice as an attending internal medicine physician, pulmonologist, and psychiatrist, I have made a connection between various body organs that must perform synchronously to develop our psyche, which plays an important role in our daily lives to keep us in balance with people; otherwise, we will be distorted mentally and physically.

You can apply these solutions to your life. Feelings are started in the heart, which is a source of wishes, desires, and curiosity. Jealousy, anger, greed, injustice, and hate are all negative feelings. Desires can be good, such as helping people, or they can be bad, such as seeking revenge or punishing or harming others.

All thoughts, which originate in the mind, pass through our heart. We often make impulsive emotional decisions, which come through our heart without wisdom. In my experience, the mind is the place of power because it generates negative or positive thinking.

Negative thinking, which I perceive to be weaknesses and various fears, causes confusion and cloudiness of thought, blurring our vision so that we cannot see the truth of or reality behind making wrong decisions. We start looking at this beautiful world through dark glasses, creating a hopeless environment around us and increasing our fear level, which leads to uncertainty and kills the feeling of doing good for humanity. The physical appearance of a negative thinker will show signs of stress, fatigue, irritability, and restless anger.

Positive thinking is the reflection of satisfaction and happiness that controls our negative behaviors and balances our desires, wishes, hate, guilt, pain, anger, and psychological illness, including anxiety and depression. Positive thinking gives us a feeling to bring brightness and happiness into our life. Teach your mind how to feel satisfaction, which leads to happiness. Start training your mind to generate energy in your body by using your positive thinking process, which leads to increased productivity in daily life. Create a feeling of thankfulness in your heart for the creator that we are living in the current century and taking advantage of technology, decent food, a better life, and a good education, which is also a blessing to further improve our lives and better serve humanity. These blessings make me more thankful and produce an internal satisfaction with what I am doing. Once you have those feelings, they will glow in your heart, and you can feel their heat in the form of energy to do more in your professional life.

It does not matter how much you are earning. You must be a king of your heart and understand how to control such demanding feelings as high status, greediness, and cheating to get money from the wrong sources to avoid frustration. The key to success is working hard with honesty and sincerity. If you do this, then soon you will get what you want. Money earned with honesty may be less in amount, but your satisfaction level will be higher than it would be if you earned the money through the wrong means. You may have a luxury life but no peace of mind. You may not be able to sleep without pills, or you may abuse drugs and alcohols. Now you can decide which pathway is good for you. The physical appearance of a positive thinker is reflected in facial expressions; glowing eyes will reflect a positive behavior and attitude toward life. Having a strong personality and self-confidence will impress others.

5. Self-management of High Expectations

This process starts very early in the brain if various events and incidences are not in our favor. Our minds set up various types of fears, more negativity, obsession, concern about our existence in the organization, and feeling sick in the mind about not doing enough or not having enough respect. When starting a new job, everyone has certain aims about that job, particularly a first job. You are enthusiastic and full of positive energy. You want to change the shape of the organization and rise to a top position. These are high expectations: a bright future, a good salary, the ability to pay education loans, and so on. Soon you gain high status in society or start working with increased motivation and commitment to achieve a lot for the organization. But after few months, you notice that the organization does not appreciate you or provide you with monitoring awards, the boss does not show verbal appreciation, and nobody cares about your suggestions or advice. People wish to be appreciated in whatever jobs they are doing. Once this realization comes to you as a highly motivated person, why would you do extra work without appreciation or awards? This is when negative feelings first start. You begin slowing down and losing interest in your job. Then you start missing deadlines or cannot keep pace with the work according to the organization's expectations. You are now starting to face an overwhelming situation, and your work productivity gradually reduces. You begin feeling stress in regard to the same job descriptions that you were previously fulfilling perfectly.

The following factors are also a hindrance in the completion of high expectations, which may begin the early burnout process: the boss may not be good; the work environment and coworkers are not good; you were hired for a specific job but are then given additional duties, with no incentives, for which you may not have the skills; you demand too much in the way of resources; your work productivity is poor; your immediate supervisor feels threatened by your very high productivity; your experience and skill are not matched with the job description; or downsizing leads to reduced resources and a smaller number of employees doing the job, which results in feelings of overload.

Whenever you or your employer has higher expectations with a lot of negativity around the workplace, you want to perform well. You will take this as a challenge and try to find your hidden abilities and skill sets to accomplish this task with a high rate of success that will add to your optimal experience and self-confidence. In this way, you must develop a readiness to accept challenges without fear of failure. As you repeat this process, you will develop outside-the-box thinking, and your mind will be ready for innovative solutions of complex issues at work and develop the ability to meet very high expectations with great success and without any negative feeling of burnout. At this stage, do not think about awards, rewards, or increased salary. The real happiness will be your internal satisfaction, which cannot be achieved with a salary increase. Do not be too materialistic. Simply wait. The time will come when the people around you recognize your efforts, and soon you will become an asset to the organization. But you have to maintain your positivity. I know some bosses are senseless; they do not care about hardworking, good employees, and they do not show appreciation for their good work. Do not take this seriously because bosses may feel that it is your job to do what you were hired to do. However, if you go the extra mile and take on challenging projects, putting in additional time to get good results, then your boss may appreciate you with some kind of monitoring awards. But do not think in this way. Think my way, which is that you are always ready take on projects and to maximize your time and efforts to accommodate new tasks and improve your efficiency for your future career—and most important, for the feeling of internal happiness that you have done something good for the organization. My philosophy is to just do it. Feel happy and add new a skill to your optimal experience by gaining a state of flow, which gives you a new kind of energy and keeps you ready for the next level. I never say no to additional work. I even sometimes ask for additional projects. Recently, my boss told me that another department needed help to meet a deadline for a large project and that the supervisor was overwhelmed, exhausted, and unable to complete the project. I immediately left my work and met with that supervisor. I spent two hours learning about the work. Although it was not relevant to my work experience, I took the responsibility and reviewed one thousand pages of financial data, which I completed in eight to ten hours. I developed a guideline for the supervisor on how to deal with this issue in time to meet the financial services deadline. After this, I felt internally satisfied that I had found a new, hidden talent to resolve this issue and to help someone prevent burnout. I noticed when dealing with this person that he was confused, anxious, panicky, overwhelmed, and unable to focus on the project, even though he had just come back from a two-week vacation. I noticed that this project was due prior to his vacation. In my experience and observation, vacations or saying no to any additional work are not helpful to prevent burnout.

I assure you that you can do this too. Relax and think about how you can split your project into various smaller components on a daily basis to avoid panic attacks. I verbally provided immediate guidelines on how various departments could play their roles in confirming charges on which I did not have the background information. In this way, my questions were resolved, and I was able to manage early burnout for many employees. In my career, I have managed several burnout victims successfully and brought them back to a normal track so that they could continue their jobs burnout-free.

When I was working in Saudi Arabia, one physician was under too much stress and anxiety, and his work performance was suffering. The hospital director was putting a lot of pressure on this physician about not doing well. I was fully aware of this and decided to help the physician. I evaluated his fear of failure and his lack of confidence in patient management as an attending physician. I provided guidance on how to reduce stress and build confidence to manage his patients so that the director stopped chasing him. After six months of psychotherapy to help him manage stress, I would personally sit in his clinic with him to reassure him that he had successfully built his self-confidence. After this, he was able to fully overcome early burnout.

6. Anger Management

Anger is the consequence of frustration, forgetfulness, and irritability due to negativity in thought processes, which due to failure of accomplishment and which can later lead to burnout. You must learn how to control anger. It is not easy. You have to be calm and relax—no knee-jerk responses. Try to understand anger from others. Put yourself in their shoes. It is always better to leave a hot environment than to further provoke anger. Go to a separate place, drink a glass of cold water, and allow your anger to gradually cool down.

7. Controlling Weaknesses and Converting Them into Strengths

Everyone has weaknesses that can include negativity about life, fear, confusion, and reduced self-confidence. Always take negativity seriously and try to find a positive angle from which to view negative issues by adding new knowledge to your hidden abilities; this will help you to think more positively. For example, when my boss tells me about my deficiency at work, instead of getting angry and developing a negative opinion of the boss, I analyze myself to see how I can improve and overcome this deficiency. No one is correct all the time. We must always be ready to accept and correct weaknesses and to convert them into strengths. Our weaknesses also lead to stress, anxiety, and fear, which can block the thinking process. Thus, you will be unable to make decisions, analyze situations, or think positively or realistically. For example, if you are reading material or important documents at work when you are under pressure or feeling tension, then you will miss several important messages or action items. When you read in this state, your eyes are looking at the words, but your mind is somewhere else, and it fails to understand the issues and to find solutions for them. All this happens when you are facing the early onset of burnout.

Strengths will lead toward perfection and will include positive thinking, positive attitude, self-confidence, unclouded vision, clear goals, and knowledge of how to implement those goals to develop new experiences and skill sets in the database of your mind. Next time, you will be ready to accept any task or challenge and to convert it into a positive outcome.

8. Stress Control

It is most important that you learn how to manage stress. It is an art. Once you understand your own personality, you may be able to find a hidden skill to tackle your stress according to the nature of the issue surrounding it, either in the workplace or in your daily life. You can first define your feelings under stress. For example, you notice (or someone told you about) your lack of attention or concentration during a talk or meeting. This may be because your mind is in the middle of a puzzle, or it's obsessed. First, trace the related factor to the stress. Sit in a calm place and analyze the situation by writing down your thoughts about the problem. Note whether it is your fault and whether you can easily fix it, or whether it needs to be taken to your supervisor. If you have a good, sincere friend who knows your nature and can understand your problem, then this person could help to resolve your issue and rebalance your emotions. This will help to control and nullify your stress. Keep in mind that this stress may have a subcomponent of hidden fear that you will be unable to recover from the issue or come out of the situation.

A Mechanistic Approach to Self-care Solution of Burnout

The majority of burnout victims have one or more of the following emotional states that must be self-corrected accordingly.

1. Apathy: Low difficulty of challenges and lack of skill set to tackle those challenges → lack of interest in the task at hand

If you feel apathy, you can combat it by using positive thinking, which entails having the intention to do your task, learn a new a skill set, and even demand a slightly more challenging task. In this situation, I also recommend asking your coworkers for help or using outside sources to develop the skill set to accomplish this task. You not only will learn something new in the process but also may even bolster your interest in doing the task.

2. Boredom: Low difficulty of challenges and skill level exceeds those challenges → boredom

I have heard from so many people who say that their jobs are boring due the low difficulty of challenges in conjunction with a skill set that exceeds the demands of their work. They feel compelled to do more, but in many cases, they simply do not have the freedom to do so, and they are not being compensated for having a higher skill set. If this is not possible, try to find intrinsic or extrinsic motivation to continue your task. Even if it does not help any particular person directly, it may make your life easier. As a very rudimentary example, if one of your tasks is to staple paper forms together for one hour at work daily, then you can perhaps take pleasure in the fact that these papers will be organized for the person who has to fill out this form, realizing that you are making this person's life easier. This is a very simple example, but I think it gets the point across. By taking this an approach, it will give you at least some motivation to develop interest in your work to continue your job. If you feel that you have the skill set to accomplish more and you have the ability to face bigger challenges, then it may be better to consider another job.

3. Worry: Somewhat challenging and low skills → chronic stress leads to burnout

If anyone has low skills and is having some challenges at workplace to accomplish a task, if it continues unresolved, that leads to chronic stress and later burnout.

4. Anxiety: Challenges high and skills low → distress and uneasiness lead to burnout

This is very common among burnout victims due to a mismatch between high challenges and low skills.

5. Relaxation: Low challenge and high skills → no burnout

The individual will enjoy and relax in the workplace, handling low-challenge tasks with a high level of skill and no burnout.

6. Control: Somewhat challenging and high skills → no burnout

The individual with high skills and mild to moderate challenging tasks will have total control at the workplace and no feeling of burnout.

7. Happiness: Challenges high and skills high → learning new skills

If challenges are too great, you can return to the flow state by learning new skills. Flow is a source of mental energy in that it focuses attention and motivates action and feelings of happiness.

How to Control or Block the Psychological Process of Burnout

Most burnout victims have one or more of the following emotional states as a late onset of burnout, and they must seek advice from a psychologist or psychiatrist:

Worthlessness à Depersonalization à Cynicism à
Detachment à Isolation à Depression à Suicide

Burnout occurs when expectations outstrip reality. Once burnout victims lose their purpose to survive (worthlessness), then negativity will take over, leading to reduced self-esteem, decreased motivation, and reduced productivity. They will begin to isolate themselves and turn to alcohol and drugs. Later, depression sets in, along with suicidal thoughts and even a suicide attempt when they feel that life is meaningless. Our minds and bodies warn us that we are facing burnout. Burnout victims are best able to identify the cause of chronic stress and inferior performance in the workplace. Burnout victims clinically present with anxiety due to chronic work-related stress; in advanced cases, they present with depression with or without suicidal thoughts. In the depression phase, feelings of job dissatisfaction decrease efficacy and reduce job performance, which leads to negative attitudes and behaviors. A chronic mismatch between employee and employer causes erosion of passion. Burnout may have a direct link to high demand and less job resources, which leads to loss of control and failure to achieve tasks on time, resulting in frustration. Personality plays a role in the burnout process and includes thinking style, lack of self-confidence, fear of failure, attitude, behavior, and environment. Finally, burnout presents as physical and emotional exhaustion, depersonalization, and low performance due to reduced productivity in the workplace. Prevention should focus on halting progression and treating the signs and symptoms of burnout. The main goal of this book is to transform negative cognitive patterns into positive cognitive patterns that will improve your perspective on life. During this phase, you must consult primary care physician, psychologist, or psychiatrist.

Recently, I met with someone who appeared to have features of burnout. He was doing research, and after general introduction, I noticed that he was overwhelmed and anxious. He stated he was worried about his performance in his classes and what the future held. In the beginning, I assumed that college was in general stressful, but my intuition guided me to dig a little deeper about his work performance. I decided to ask permission to evaluate him because I thought he was having early burnout features. He agreed and opened up to me. I started the process of my evaluation as discussed in the beginning of this chapter and took a good history and clinical exam. I asked him to do the self-assessment from my primary care physician screening tool questionnaire for early diagnosis of burnout. He scored 70 out of 100 points, and on the second self-assessment, for late onset diagnosis of burnout, he scored 39 out of 100. It confirmed my final diagnoses of burnout, and if untreated, it would turn into late onset. His college performance was dropping, and he described "a general haziness" of his thoughts. Even simple things like cooking and cleaning were becoming difficult to perform. His thoughts were preoccupied with the fear of failure, and his confidence in his own abilities wavered. He was unsure whether he would have a job by the end of college or whether he would even be any good at the job. It seemed to have started suddenly because he had entered his final year of college and didn't recall being an anxious or depressed person.

In my evaluation, he was approaching the late stage of burnout. I recommended he consult his primary care physician (PCP) to get selective serotonin reuptake inhibitors (SSRIs) to begin treatment; he should follow you're his PCP's instructions. After seeing his doctor, he started treatment with a low dose and then gradually increased the dose for optimal results. Treatment went on for two to three months. I met him again after six weeks, and he was happy to get a correct diagnosis and treatment. Now he is back to feeling almost normal. He feels motivated with self-confidence and has increasing clarity of mind. He has become more task oriented to complete his day-to-day educational activities. This example will help you be confident that if you are suffering from burnout, there is successful treatment available to help you get back to your normal life.

Chapter 8

Prevention of Future Burnout

In my personal experience, expectations often do not fit with work-life balance, lead to increase compensation, or underscore a lack of confidence in your ability to tackle challenges. This leads to negative thinking, which reduces energy and decreases motivation, thus resulting in the early onset of burnout. During my first residency in urology, I was working for thirty-six hours straight at the hospital, with twelve hours in between for eating, sleeping, and living the rest of my life. I did this for one year with no time off. I balanced this overwhelming and stressful situation by keeping alive my self-motivation to learn the best patient care from my professor and building my self-confidence to tackle critical patients who were in life-and-death situations. I tried to deliver the best possible quality care in order to gain faith in my abilities to be the best doctor I could be in the future. These thoughts were good enough for me to prevent burnout by handling challenges and adversities with positive thinking and sacrificing time and sleep to be the best physician I could. I spent eight years in various medical and surgical departments and residencies as well as family practice. I did postgraduate work in pulmonary medicine and practiced as an attending physician and pulmonologist at a psychiatric hospital to exclude medical illness from psychiatry illness. In this way, I developed a command of psychiatry illnesses, diagnoses, and treatments.

This exposure taught me to become a good attending physician and psychiatrist to confidently manage patients.

I did not suffer from severe burnout due to my personal positive thinking and attitude, self-motivation to provide maximum comfort to all patients, and self-confidence and desire to sacrifice my time, sleep, and money for my patients. This gave me a sense of internal happiness and self-satisfaction, knowing that whatever I was doing, I was doing it for my patients. Then there was no place for frustration or exhaustion in my life. I have faced a lot of workplace issues that could have developed into the early onset of burnout, but I tackled them according to my personality and my ability to sacrifice money and personal time. From this, I gained self-satisfaction and internal happiness. With strong determination, I converted my goals into 100 percent positive outcomes by making the implausible plausible. My mind and heart learned to survive in adverse situations and environments due to my outside-the-box thinking to find innovative solutions to problems. These qualities will make you burnout-proof as well as a strong and confident leader who finds success within the organization and within your life. You must follow my lead to make and implement positive changes in your personality and be a good human being.

While working as an attending physician and pulmonologist and director in Saudi Arabia, I had barely one day off in two weeks for about six years, but I had forty-five days of annual leave. I survived by changing my mind-set to find satisfaction in my work no matter the obstacles. For me, burnout comes from the inability to take responsibility for the work, irritability, and so on.

Critical thinking should be built from an early age and should be the responsibility of school and college teachers. This will help students tackle the stresses they will face in life, such as death of relatives, divorce, and cancer. Stress management should be part of our education curriculum. Try to assess your personality and generate positive thinking toward work and life. Seek help from friends who are positive thinkers rather than discussing these issues with unreliable or less experienced people who cannot give you good advice.

Parents' Role in Developing Childhood Personality to Prevent Future Burnout

Since childhood, due to learning from my parents, I was ambitious and dreamed to be successful through hard work and honesty and by accomplishing goals with a clear vision and intrinsic motivation. I was energetic, passionate, able to make quick decisions, strong willed, independent, self-sufficient, holistic, confident, stimulated, unemotional, resilient, and decisive, all of which led me to immediately correct wrong things, lead change, systematize everything (including a goal or target), and be highly focused on work. I was also outstanding in math, and therefore, I am more analytical, logical, and pragmatic, quickly figuring out issues and their solutions. I rely on my own logic and reasoning, investigate facts on my own, and am vigilant in my progress on projects. I am highly independent and set high standards, and I am also diligent, hardworking, rarely satisfied, and persistent. My nature is organization and seeing a smooth pattern in system development.

I demonstrated my thoughtfulness at various organizations where I worked by analyzing problems that were too difficult for others. I also have my eye on the negative attributes of life. I am self-reliant and independent, and I get wholly involved in what I am doing. I am highly creative in activities that make a significant and lasting difference in the organization. I am always ready to self-sacrifice. I am very introspective and hold myself to a high standard. I have the ability to finish projects on time, and I am schedule oriented and detail conscious. I see the problem and suggest creative solutions with ease. I am very competitive and forceful. I am focused on maintaining excellent work habits and keep after details until the job is completely finished.

I have highly intrinsic motivation, which provides me with reasons for actions, desires, and needs. This drives me to seek new things and new challenges and analyze my own capacity to observe and gain knowledge.

There are many parts of my life that I enjoy, including listening to music, cooking a meal for parties or family members, cleaning and decorating, gardening, minor home repairs, spending time with my family, and reading a book or watching political news and discussions on television. These are my self-contained activities that allow me to enjoy life because I set targets for my daily activities and allow myself to gain more positive energy. Many consider it boring. Nearly every day, I remain fully absorbed in my projects and love what I am doing. I have been practicing these activities since my childhood, and now they are part of who I am. Anyone can evaluate oneself through observation to determine whether one has the characteristics to achieve success.

According to my experience, if you have the following basic capabilities, then you have the makings of a good leader and can help prevent burnout among other leaders: setting self-targets in daily life, achieving targets, self-rewarding credit, becoming fully absorbed in achieving targets, losing sense of time, feelings of self-enjoyment and relaxation, learning new skills during this process, gaining more confidence, and being ready to accept new challenges in life, at home, and at work.

It is my curiosity and desire to learn on a daily basis from others, even from my kids, and to adapt to new situations and new ideas; it does not matter from where they come. I am action oriented, have high hopes for success, and have no fear of failure. I am ready to accept failure and dig into its causes to immediately correct myself and be ready for new challenges. I think I have total control of and confidence in my abilities, and I have developed a high rate of performing acts for intrinsic reasons due to my internal drive. I am not influenced by money, prestige, and other environmental factors. I am willing to learn new things that enhance my skill and confidence on a daily basis. It also enhances my self-esteem and leaves me anxiety-free.

I have both physical and mental energy to achieve my daily targets at work and at home and to improve my skills on a daily basis. I use my positive psychology on a daily basis to perform an activity with 100 percent feeling of energized focus, full involvement, and enjoyment in the process. These kinds of activities lead to happiness in my life.

I have learned to see how far I can stretch to accept maximum challenges in my life with a high efficacy rate and without any stress. We have to learn enjoyment while we accomplish a job with happiness without being bored. Do not care about those around you who may have asked why you are doing so much without a raise or awards. In my mind, everything I am doing is just for my happiness. I feel very happy after helping people; therefore, I have no frustration.

Creating Strong, Confident Leaders

In my opinion, we have to teach others to find their leadership qualities, potential hidden talents, and skill sets to perform well in daily and professional life. This education should take place in schools, colleges, universities, and during medical training so that everyone can learn how to self-analyze their personalities and make clear, strong decisions to brighten their careers. I think we each have these basic foundations to fight chronic stress and negativity with positive energy and attitude. I think that a passionate state of mind and self-confidence as informed intuition make the best kind of leader in any field.

Your success is hidden in your positive thinking. Be optimistic and selfless, and do not seek external rewards or glory. Keep your expectations low to prevent frustration and balance negative feelings. Try to think and do good for everyone to generate feelings of internal satisfaction. Once you succeed in achieving these qualities, you have less chance of burnout. You try to accept smaller tasks to generate focus and clarity of mind for how you will accomplish good results. Each good result gives you confidence and builds your career on a solid foundation where you do not fear failure and have faith in your abilities. These habits will lead to your success as a person and as an efficient doctor or leader.

I firmly believe that self-management will help you control negative thinking by blocking early symptoms of burnout as you work to address the causes of burnout at a personal level. It is a fundamental approach to learning how to make positive changes in your psychology related to working at a fast pace in a time-sensitive, high-risk, high-pressure environment so that you can avoid stress and exhaustion. Do this by keeping a positive attitude, which is a reflection of positive thinking with positive energy. How you can develop these abilities? Accept extra projects or tasks as challenges to meet the demands of the organization. There is nothing wrong if the organization benefits from you. Do not be selfish. In this way, you will try to unlock the cause to prevent future burnout.

Usually, burnout will start with your own belief system and thinking in a negative way that the organization is not paying you enough and your workload is high. This is the point when stress is sparked. If it is not blocked by a positive approach, it will become chronic. Usually the word *chronic* is used for any symptoms that will continue for more than six months. Once symptoms become chronic, they are difficult to revert.

My philosophy is to just do it. Do not be selfish. Volunteer. Develop flexibility in your thinking and attitude. Try to develop a way of doing things for others so that you can start feeling internal happiness. Do not pay attention to extra money for extra work.

How can you avoid negative thinking? Let's consider this example. An organization plans to downsize to save money and use employees in a more productive way. When you hear about these plans, it sounds like a scary situation. If you are a negative thinker, you will stress that you will be doing extra work for the same salary. You are not thinking that you are getting a chance to take on additional responsibilities, learn new techniques, and gain new experiences to find your hidden talents and skill sets. In this way, you may be able to bring new talents to the surface that can enhance your abilities in a new field or area of work experience. I notice that most people feel irritated and exhausted when they are promoted to an acting or interim position because they are mentally not ready to accept this position and believe they will do additional work without compensation. They are too materialistic. If you are promoted to an acting position, it is a blessing according to my thinking because this is the best opportunity to show your potential with positive outcomes. Remember to always keep your self-motivation at a high level so that you can meet all deadlines and gradually improve your time management. In this way, you will tackle an increased workload with a positive attitude.

If, due to downsizing, reduced resources, or work overload, you go into the stress phase, negative thinking will decrease your energy and lead you to the next level of exhaustion; now you are approaching burnout. Your confidence will decrease, you'll fear failure, your vision will be cloudy, you'll have reduced faith in your abilities, and you'll develop feelings of worthlessness.

Burnout has its own belief system, workload, sense of control, rewards, community, fairness, and value. It includes the boss treating you unfairly, a heavy workload burden, no sense of joy or fulfillment, and an empty feeling inside.

Negative feelings and thoughts are major killers of your personality. They will decrease your confidence, prevent you from managing goals (even small daily targets), and lead to depression, detachment, and inefficiency in society. If these feelings continue, they will lead to depression and may develop into suicidal thoughts.

Positive Thinking Leads to Intrinsic Motivation: The Path to Pleasure and Happiness to Prevent Burnout

The negative thoughts cause stress and various types of fear (such as losing your job or being diagnosed with an untreatable illness or death) that can make us unhappy from time to time. We obsess about the majority of our negative thoughts while at the same time TV news channels spread negative news around the globe, which further increases our stress level. Very rarely do we hear positive news, which is like a breath of a fresh air. Then our minds start telling us there is still some hope to make this world a good place and that there are still good people around us.

I decided to write this book to help those who are or will be victims of burnout. I started collecting memories of my life as a doctor and the various phases of disappointments, hardships, and stresses I experienced. In my opinion, everybody's life is full of various types of worries and includes a high rate of negativities. It is necessary for us all to assess our mental status from time to time. It requires some practice, as well as application of intrinsic motivation, to learn how to self-evaluate. Remember, early detection is the cure for many illnesses. Sometimes our negative thoughts are painful and produce strong emotions that lead to fear.

With this book, you will learn how you can control negative thoughts and then convert them into positive thoughts. When you engage in an abundance of positive thinking, then you reflect peace of mind, more self-confidence, internal happiness, and clarity of mind and goals, which will create a feeling of well-being and self-awareness. That is the key element to preventing depersonalization and detachment, two feelings that are a part of burnout.

Positive thinking can prevent burnout, but it is only part of the solution. In my opinion, negative thinking leads to frustration, fatigue, and loss of energy and motivation to continue achieving tasks in order to improve work performance. The end result is burnout. This means that negative thinkers are more prone to burnout due to reduced efficiency at work because negative thoughts and feeling are dominant in these people.

We are all born with several weaknesses that develop into various types of fears, create more and more negativity in our thinking and attitude, and lead to irritability and anxiety. Some fears that I believe we all have are a fear of failure at relationships, a fear of failing in school or being unable to keep grades up, and a fear of failing in business. I can easily identify people who engage in negative thinking. For example, if you say, "Good morning," then the person will say, "What is good this morning?" This means the negative-thinking person will see every moment of life through dark glasses and will be unable to see the beauty around us. So many people are obsessed with personal health issues. Negative thinkers are always very comfortable talking with other like-mind people—that is, the same type of negative people. In this way, they will get sympathy from other negative thinkers and feel comfortable that these people are also suffering. At the end of the day, they all end up with more negative feelings. They feel enjoyment when other people are suffering, and they do not like to connect with positive-thinking people so that they cannot improve. Sometimes these negative people get angry with me when I try to teach them how to convert their negativity into positivity. They have told me that their lives are miserable due to their illnesses and that I cannot feel their suffering. Some extreme negative thinkers are mentally preoccupied with obsession and fear of failure. They have no motivation or confidence and feel lazy all the time, so they fail to meet deadlines and make many errors at work. They cannot pay attention or concentrate. They are unable to focus. Some of these components of negative feelings lead to frequent burnout, causing the person to totally lose control.

How can you convert negative thinking to positive thinking? In my opinion, first you must learn to identify negative thinking, as in the examples just described. Then you must try to control your negative thinking. This will take some time. Write down your weaknesses in priority order. Imagine that all your negative thinking is your weakness. You need not worry or become overwhelmed or stressed because all human beings are the same. Everyone is born with various weaknesses. We must learn how we can control our weaknesses. Once we control them, we can work to convert them into strengths. Once you reach a level of strength, you will gain self-confidence, which leads to success and happiness in life.

Life is all about continuous learning and finding ways to improve one's weaknesses.

If you deeply analyze your negative thinking, you will find an underlying hidden fear. You can overcome this deficiency by changing your thinking style and attitude and becoming more realistic and honest when evaluating yourself. Doing this will allow you to find a new angle for betterment so that you can twist negativity and weakness into positivity and strength. It takes some mental agility to find ways to adapt to new changes.

With daily practice, you will be able to identify negative thinking, and once it's identified, you will be able to control it. When you learn to control it, then you will start gaining strength in your body. Our minds need training. If you engage in negative thinking, then immediately switch your mind-set and bring out the good things from those negative thoughts.

When a task is given to negative thinkers, they will often say, "I cannot do this. It is impossible for me. How can I do it alone? I have no energy or plan in my mind to finish it." In response, I remember my mother saying, "Salar, nothing is impossible. You can do it. I am sure you can do it alone and with perfection because I have seen your dedication and interest in performing a task. You know how to deal with challenges. You will face a lot of challenges in your life." After this reassurance from my mother, I gained more confidence and energy. My positive thinking process expanded, and my mind generated new ideas and thoughts to push my energy level higher and awaken my mind to divergent thinking. In the beginning, my mother told me to do a task according to her guidelines, but once I experienced divergent thinking, I realized there were various ways to do projects and tasks. This way, your goal will become easier to achieve, you will meet your deadline, and your time management will improve, which leads to success. Prior to sleep, you must make it a practice to think about the day's activities as positive outcomes to enhance and strengthen your positive thinking.

We must learn to avoid anger by engaging in positive thinking. For example, if the boss is angry with you for not meeting a deadline, then apologize, relax, and calm down. Next, think of your boss's perspective instead of your own. You will probably realize the boss was right. Then there is no need for anger. You must correct yourself and continue to move in a positive direction. Do not waste your energy on obsessing over negative thoughts about your boss. We are all human, and everyone has a job to do, whether at work, home, or school. In this way, you will not react abnormally. This is the real test of keeping your positive attitude. Even if it is not my fault, I will say sorry and move on because I will not pollute the remainder of my day with stress and frustration. I always finish my work and go home with great happiness to enjoy time with my family and benefit from a restful sleep so that I am ready for the next day. It is not impossible; it requires only a positive approach to any issue or problem. In time, you will be able to manage yourself under worse circumstances. Some people have irritating personalities or bad mouths, or they provoke you to an immediate reaction. This is the time to show maturity, calmness, and discipline. Avoid any clash or wrongdoing, such as road rage or fighting, and avoid harming someone. The bottom line is to relax, ignore, learn to forgive, and put yourself into the other person's shoes. Maybe that person is having family or job-related issues, or the person is suffering from a chronic illness that causes irritability. If you are healthy, are well-to-do, and do not have any problems in your personal life, why not forgive and give the person another chance?

Surround Yourself with Positive Thinkers

When you talk to someone, your mind starts processing to assess the other person's attitude toward life or other surroundings, including those at work or things related to finance and studies. Remember that some negative th inkers always focus on their own issues and health, whereas positive thinkers listen more, quickly analyze the other person, and give short but strong solutions to the issues, which stem from clarity of mind and quick decision-making abilities. You can feel positive energy emanating from this person.

I recommend that positive thinkers find negative people and try their best to convince them to convert their negativity to positivity. Don't worry if you are not successful; you did your best. Find something that helps you relax, like long drives, eating out, talking with a like-mind friend, watching a good movie, or anything that is recreational and that provides a feeling of fun. Relaxing in this way will keep you ready to tackle another challenge in life without any negativity. Life is a healthy, pleasant thing that is used for serving humanity to avoid stress. Please do not make your life complicated, full of disputes and enemies. Try to distribute love only so that people have enough time to correct their mistakes and realize what is wrong. Most people, including me, do not recognize their faults, bad attitudes, or complaints. But now that I have corrected myself, I am living a happy life and love my job. Always keep your life and home environments peaceful, and do not engage in status competitions with friends, relatives, and neighbors. I know my financial status; there is no need to compete with anyone in a negative way. It is my life. I need to know how I can keep myself happy with healthy competition through education and hard work so that I can progress positively and without any negative feelings. I assure you it will give you sound sleep and peace of mind. Try to earn money with honesty, without any wrongdoing or cheating. In this way, you can accumulate or generate a lot of money and gain high status in society. There will be no problem because you will continue with positive thinking, which is a blessing and will give you internal satisfaction. For me, internal happiness is the bottom line, and I feel that I am the happiest man on earth.

I always try to learn from other people's mistakes and correct myself to implement a remedial plan in my life so that if similar situations arise, I will find myself ready. Negative or horrible news is part of the world and can make us sad and anxious, but this news helps me to think about why it is happening and who is responsible for acts of terror, shootings, and drugs. Why aren't our leaders trying to correct our living environment to reduce these events?

Please do not discuss your personal issues and problems with everyone, because people may give you the wrong advice, which will further damage your thinking and attitude toward wrongdoing. You must try to pick one sincere and honest friend who listens to you, understands your weaknesses, and gives proper advice for your betterment, as opposed to spoiling your life by giving you the wrong advice. Love yourself, love your job, and love your family to get maximum peace of mind and prevent burnout.

The key to my success is accepting challenges and taking on more projects without any additional salary to improve my skill set to prevent burnout. Wherever I have worked, I have always performed duties beyond my job description and have taken on additional responsibilities for the betterment of the organization and my internal happiness.

I have a career path as a doctor that requires special training and comes with some expectation of progress throughout the course of a person's life. A job is an activity that someone performs in exchange for payment, whereas work is an activity that someone performs to produce or accomplish something. Work is a general term that refers to all activities that one does; job is more specific. When you are hired for a job, you have a contract with your employer and must abide by the regulations of the company.[16]

In a job, the goals and targets are more specific and are well laid out for the employees to follow and achieve. This may lead to chronic stress and burnout. This is very common due to a mismatch between high challenges and low skills, such as physicians who have low skill with patients' electronic medical records. Spending too much time on them is overwhelming and can raise stress levels.

[16] Salar A. Khan, *Unlocking the Natural-Born Leader's Abilities: An Autobiographical Exposé* (Bloomington, IN: Xlibris, 2018), 77–80.

The term *daily basis* is common and refers to the activities we perform to achieve a desired outcome. Most people understand that the meaning of a job is to come in for a certain period of time and complete the tasks in their job description so that they earn a regular salary and are not fired. Some employees are not flexible, never volunteer for additional work, and hesitate to participate in change unless additional compensation will be offered.

In my opinion, these people are not successful in their career paths, whereas people like me come to work to accomplish daily targets both inside and outside an official job without any thought of compensation for work and time. I never asked to be compensated for my personal time to achieve the goal of research program accreditation at the Jesse Brown VA Medical Center in 2005, and I also set an example of volunteering my personal time to work for the hospital under the Saudi Arabia Ministry of Health, holding additional top positions in the hospital besides doing my regular job as an attending physician and pulmonologist, treating inpatients and outpatients as well as those in the ICU and ER. I never asked for compensation but instead accepted additional responsibilities in the hospital administration to gain self-confidence and learn a new skill that was hidden inside me. This was a good chance to work in a highly responsible position to discover my hidden talents and build my self-confidence so I could deal with risk management as a hospital administrator answerable to the Saudi Arabia Ministry of Health without any additional salary.

These were the days when I enjoyed authority, treating patients, dealing with nurses and hospital staff (including doctors, the patient relations department, and Saudi and non-Saudi staff), and maintaining balance and justice with all hospital employees. I was conducting six high-level meetings as chair and dealing with daily hospital activities. I remember that I never thought that I was doing a job; I treated it broadly as work. I was working toward a vision for the sake of the hospital and my internal satisfaction in order to provide the best care to suffering patients. This was important to me, so I was flexible and would do anything to maintain that vision. This started after my medical residency in Pakistan and followed to my later work in Saudi Arabia and now in the United States. Throughout this, I was always in a state of flow and felt a self-rewarding force within me. In my opinion, the feeling I got is indescribable, and even if I got a million dollars, it would not make me as happy as the feeling of value I receive when I help suffering human beings, making a contribution toward them and enhancing the organization's reputation. I am glad to say I am doing work at the Jesse Brown VA Medical Center that is beyond my job description. I know how I can find additional time to achieve several targets on a daily basis.

Burnout results from a combination of factors. It is best understood by considering the individual, interpersonal, and organizational factors that contribute to the condition. Recognizing the causes of burnout can itself be a step in dealing with and preventing burnout. A few include the following.

+ Doing daily tasks with some variation to make them meaningful. This keeps you interested in continuing your job and avoiding a boring situation.
+ Doing your job without any appreciation or positive response from others because you are doing the job to earn for your own survival.
+ Avoiding negative thinking due to a lack of accomplishment. If you have a weakness due to a deficiency in a skill required for your job, then you are on the losing end of stress and burnout.
+ Realizing that prolonged workplace tension will deteriorate your well-being; it is better to look for another job where you will feel comfortable.
+ Realizing that if you work with a difficult supervisor and cannot manage your workload, then it is better to change jobs.

Chapter 9

Teaching Stress-Control Management and Internal Happiness

In this modern computerized era, we multitask at work and accomplish our goals in a shorter period of time and with accuracy while meeting deadlines and using our time management skills to meet our daily demands. If you do not know how to perform your job, or if you lack the skill to meet daily challenges, you will be left behind and feel overloaded with work. This is the beginning of stress and includes tension, pressure, feeling overwhelmed, and becoming occupied with negative feelings of work. You then start blaming others, which leads to early burnout. Now you must think about changing your strategies to perform well at work and reduce stress. Workplace stress is increasing day by day due to greater pressure to perform, increasing demand due to technological advances, toxic work environments, and job insecurity. These all directly influence your physical, psychological, and emotional health and can affect your productivity when these symptoms keep you away from work.

How can we reduce workplace stress to improve employee health and well-being? Bosses must design manageable workloads according to demand and timeline in advance so that employees can accomplish tasks according to their skill level and knowledge. Excellent communication guides employees. Check in with employees about progress. If there are any difficulties in executing the task, be ready to help employees tackle the work to prevent feelings of being overwhelmed and exhausted.

Bosses need time to assess the available resources and create an accommodating work environment. Do not forget to appreciate and reassure employees who are struggling; this will boost their motivation and confidence to attain positive results without any further stress. We all need reassurance from our supervisors from time to time that we are doing well, gaining optimal work experience, and creating new skill sets that will be beneficial in building employees' careers and preparing the future generation of leadership. New unskilled employees learn from their bosses. If the boss is hardworking and sincere, has good communication skills, provides clear instructions, and spends time with employees, then employees will feel relaxed and stress-free. They will not fear asking the boss about anything on which they need more clarification to quickly complete a task. I believe that the main cause of early onset burnout is due to employees with self-conflicts—those who do not have the skills needed to finish the job, have no prior experience, or are too shy to ask questions about how to do things at work, which leads to unforeseen consequences. Overcoming these conflicts keeps unnecessary stress from entering your life through your workplace. If you are unable to resolve your workplace issues or are not motivated enough to put forth the extra effort needed to quickly learn new things, then perhaps it is better to look for another job that matches your experience.

Time Management Prevents Stress

Make it a habit to accept challenges, take on extra responsibilities, and put a sincere effort into getting positive outcomes by splitting tasks into smaller units to avoid overwhelming situations and prevent stress. Reassure yourself that you can do it to build faith in your abilities. Achieving positive results will build your self-confidence and you will be less stressful in your workplace environment. You will now enjoy challenges and prevent burnout. I followed the same path, and with continuous hard work, I achieved strong leadership roles in big organizations. Wherever I started working, I began with minimal skill and polished myself to gain optimal experiences and make innovative decisions. At this level, you will start enjoying your work with internal happiness.

Workplace stress was never discussed at school or college. You have to be motivated to learn from your early workplace experiences. I was lucky that in my childhood, my parents gave me various tasks related to daily home cleaning, helping in the kitchen, and gardening. I had a designated time to complete my tasks, and my supervisor was my mother, who excelled in time management and domestic chores. This was an opportunity to perfect my time management skills, and to this day I have never faced issues related to time management. I consistently complete my projects at least two to three weeks ahead and with a 100 percent positive outcome.

Conflict Resolution Prevents Stress

If there is any workplace conflict regarding colleagues, bosses, work-load, or lack of resources, or if you do not have the skills to handle a project, then ask for help. Make sure to resolve this conflict as soon as possible. Conflict resolution provides peace of mind and will keep you from experiencing stress and burnout.

Everyone has diverse ways to relax, which is good for preventing stress in the first place. It also depends on individual personalities. If you are an extrovert and enjoy outings, parties, and vacations, make sure that by engaging in these activities you are not taking stress with you. Otherwise you will not relax, and when you are back at work, your stress level will be high. You will be frustrated and anxious because of a heavy workload.

You may benefit from a couple of meetings with a psychologist to get tips on how to manage stress and gain the most out of your relaxation so that you can focus on your work and enhance your emotional well-being, sleep habits, and work performance. Follow a healthy lifestyle; this will reduce your risk of anxiety, depression, and burnout.

Now you will be able to self-manage stress by quickly evaluating triggering factors and deleting them from your thoughts to prevent any kind of stress from starting.

Get support from family, friends, and coworkers. If necessary, seek professional help to control your stress level as a first step to preventing early burnout.

Stress Management Prevents Burnout in General Workplace Population and Health-care Professionals

Stress control programs must focus on cognitive behavioral techniques that have proven to be very effective in preventing and treating burnout in health-care professionals. A combination of psychotherapy and regular follow-up sessions will focus on issues that arise and that must be addressed to avoid the negative thinking that can provoke burnout. Moreover, group methods are both more cost effective and more beneficial than individual counseling.

This program will also address stress reactions, self-awareness, emotional exploration, breathing exercises, and psychoeducation to improve well-being and quality of life, which can be effective with medical students and residents.

The Relationship among Stress, Fear, and Negative Thinking

The negative thoughts are enough to obsess our minds around the clock. Those who have experienced bad pasts, with several incidences and mental traumas, have significantly more negative feelings associated with stress, such as fear of losing a job, untreated illness, or death, which can cause them to be unhappy all the time. Our surroundings are overloaded with negative events and news. If there is any good news, then we feel that we are living in a fresh environment with a few moments of happiness and some positive feelings about life. Life is full of worries, hardships, disappointments, and stresses. If these continue indefinitely, they lead to mental exhaustion with no motivation to live. Learn how to control your mind to expel negativity. For example, every day at work, we may meet many people with different personalities, or we may work in poisonous environments that create a lot of negative thoughts and stresses. The best way that I expell negativity is to forgive everyone who has done me wrong. My mother instructed me in this as a child, and I have been practicing it since. Do not pay attention to useless things in life because you have certain goals to achieve in your life, and you should not waste your energy responding to them. In this way, you will not have stress or negative feelings, you can keep your positive attitude all the time, and you can focus on your target of life or fulfill job needs with definite outcomes while preserving your time-management skills. You will be highly productive and will not suffer from frustration or fear of failure. It will always prevent burnout. You can achieve a work-life balance.

Find a way to become more self-aware so that you can reduce negative thoughts and decrease sudden sadness, irritability, and anxiety by analyzing their immediate cause. If you have a solution, apply it; otherwise, do not waste your time continuing to think negatively and develop stress. Avoid obsessing over negativity; try to break it by changing your thinking toward positive events and pleasurable life moments, all while remaining motivated and energetic. Train your mind daily to focus more on the positives of life and see the beautiful and honest people around us. Feel their positive energy and use it to build a desire to be happy and internally satisfied and to sleep soundly. Always take a positive view at work: even in negative remarks about job performance, you can find some positive aspect to improve. Do not get upset about it. Truth is best. Always try to make feedback sweet by accepting mistakes and learning from them.

Keep your life simple. Eat simple and keep your clothes simple. You are not competing with the world. You have to keep your heart happy without harming anyone. Share happy moments of life with friends and family. Enjoy the beauty of humanity, nature, and life. If you relax by writing, write poetry or stories or write your memoir; it may be beneficial for other like-minded people. Always give time to serve humanity and generate feelings of self-happiness. It is the greatest pleasure of life.

Internal Happiness

The following excerpt is taken from my book *Unlocking the Natural-Born Leader's Abilities: An Autobiographical Exposé.*[16]

> In looking back on my career and accomplishments, I believe I would not be the person I am today if it weren't for my parents. My father would come home after working a long day to sit down and practice mathematics and English with me from 1964 to 1969. So, thank you for showing me what hard work looks like, for showing me that nothing comes easy, and for showing me that countless hours of hard work really do pay off.
>
> I would also like to thank my mother for teaching me how to become a respectable, professional, and well-rounded individual. Whether I was helping her with cooking or cleaning, I thank my mother for making me realize that I'm worth everything in this world.
>
> My parents gave me the strength to stand up for myself and expect nothing less than the very the best, showing me true love in its rarest form, what it feels like, and how it can extend beyond life's obstacles and challenges.

My parents taught me to have a clear goal before starting an activity and to have the self-confidence to complete a task. This leads to success, producing a feeling of internal pleasure and happiness.

All human beings are created weak, with few strengths. The few strengths we got transfer through our genes from generation to generation. Everyone is born equal. Our childhood homes and neighborhood environments have a lifelong effect on our personalities. Kids observe and then learn from their parents and other siblings at home. In my experience, kids have visual memories, and they remember all kinds of good and bad events of life from childhood, which lead to strong or weak personalities in the future. Any significant trauma in childhood may last until death and take the form of various fears and poor decision-making skills.

In the beginning, kids play with other neighborhood kids who may belong to various age groups. This is when kids learn good or bad habits. At home, if parents are aggressive, abusing, fighting, unorganized, or not spending time with their kids, it means they are spoiling future generations. If both parents are working and employ a babysitter to watch the kids, this should not be a replacement for the parents. At least one parent should spend time with the kids at night, telling real moral stories to help them develop innovative, abstract thinking; that way, children can become intellectual thinkers in the future with clarity of mind. Parents are responsible for building confidence in kids by encouraging and reassuring them that they are doing well. If kids make a mistake or error, do not scold them. Instead, sit with them and explain how to correct a mistake and to improve their focus to avoid the mistake in the future. We commit mistakes when we are distracted, and if kids do not learn how to improve their focus, then repeated errors start shaking their confidence and developing confusion, thus reducing clarity of mind. If parents notice their kids making mistakes, they must teach them to correct those mistakes. Reassurance is important when building confidence. Start by telling your children, "You can do it. It is not impossible, and you know how you can make it possible. Practice will make you perfect." Everyone makes mistakes in life, and then they learn from their mistakes. Teach children how to analyze their mistake, split it into smaller units, and think about how to do it again with a better way to achieve perfection.

These mechanisms start building self-confidence and more clarity regarding how to achieve daily targets or tasks like homework. Take any task as a challenge, think how to get positive results, praise yourself when you achieve something good, and tell your heart that you are good. You can do anything you want with a positive outcome. This will give you internal happiness, enhance your intrinsic motivation to generate high-octane energy, and refresh your body and mind. Parents should give some task at home, such as cleaning and organization, to lead to the development of time-management skills. Once kids have developed organizational and time management skills, the result is self-confidence and self-motivation, and they become target achievers at school, at college, and at work. I am 100 percent sure they will never have burnout in their lives if they practice these behaviors. They will find hidden talents and skill sets to manage workloads with a high success rate and with no fear of failure, always ready to choose challenging tasks to receive an optimal experience. They will go in a state of flow, which is a hyperfocused situation, while handling challenging tasks. Once the target is achieved, you feel internal happiness and no fatigue because you have spent several hours or days absorbed in it without noticing passing time, hunger, or other bodily needs. Once you achieve this level, you will feel like the happiest person on earth; not even a million dollars can give that kind of happiness. In my career, I went through a state of flow hundreds and thousands time. Every time, I was ready to take on additional projects at work and at home and have a real feeling of happiness, with sound sleep every day. The state of flow model (the secret to happiness) was first described by Mihaly Csikszentmihalyi.[17]

---

[17] Mihaly Csikszentmihalyi, *Flow: The Psychology of Optimal Experience* (New York: Harper & Row, 1990).

Chapter 10

Discussion and Conclusion

Discussion

Burnout is a chain reaction, similar to any kind of chemical reaction in the laboratory. It is a process, and it can be prevented or ameliorated depending on the person's attitude and personality. Preventing burnout requires self-knowledge and self-awareness. Early detection offers better control or cure of a disease or psychological changes in the mind. Brain chemistry can be altered if burnout becomes serious and lead to a mood disorder such as depression. This eventually leads to the late onset of symptoms of burnout.

Burnout is a psychological illness that deteriorates work-life balance. It is a multifactorial and multidimensional issue that must be addressed as early as possible with a definite orientation plan at the workplace related to the identification of the early onset of symptoms. In the beginning, burnout can start with simple things like workload, work schedule, lack of resources, unclear job expectations, feelings of loss of control, and work-life imbalance, which may lead to alcoholism and drug dependence. Early diagnosis and treatment are still the best option for the best prognosis. To tackle burnout, you must learn to prioritize your work and understand your limits. Life is full of situational stresses that may be beyond your control. Always be grateful for the things that you have and practice positive thinking to deal with any kind of stress.

Burnout is a slow and multifactorial process. You must learn time management to balance expectations and reality. You must work within the constraints of reality; it will protect you against the flare-up of your burnout, which can damage your personality and quality of life forever. Remember that burnout can occur to anyone and at any time. No job is ideal. A job will not always meet your expectations, and the reality will turn into a bad dream. What happens next is a chemical chain reaction in your mind that spirals into depression and possibly suicide. Employee expectations include good working hours, manageable workload, good working environment, good salary, good benefits, vacation time, job security, respect, and the resources needed to achieve workplace goals. It is the disconnect between reality and expectations that leads to burnout. Prevention is always better than a cure. Employer should implement an effective program to prevent burnout at the individual level because the precipitating causes of burnout may vary from person to person. In this way, we will provide customized care by reducing work hours, instituting frequent short breaks, banning overtime, creating balance between work and life, providing training in time management, and offering ways to cope with stress and to manage it in the future. Relaxation techniques must also be taught, along with the promotion of fitness to maintain good health. All this also requires support from colleagues, friends, and family. Provide guidance to improve sleep and diet and avoid the exhaustion factor of burnout. For advanced cases of burnout, psychiatric evaluation is essential to prevent a burnout disaster. All employees feels frustrated with and frazzled by their jobs from time to time.

Burnout is a slow, progressive condition induced by chronic stress that is characterized by emotional or physical exhaustion, cynicism, and a lack of professional efficacy. All researchers are agreed on these findings. Psychoanalyst Herbert J. Freudenberger coined the term *burnout* in 1974. He defined burnout as "the extinction of motivation or incentive, especially where one's devotion to a cause or relationship fails to produce the desired results."[18] Another psychologist, Christina Maslach, has studied burnout since the early 1980s and has created the widely used Maslach Burnout Inventory (MBI). She found that burnout occurs when certain areas of our lives are chronically mismatched with our belief systems.[19]

The following are the causes of negative thinking that must be controlled or balanced so that these emotions do not dominate our minds: frustration with excessive workload, sense of lack of control, no recognition at work or a lack of external rewards, a lack of community support, feelings of unfairness, and feeling no value at work. For me, all these elements lead to the development of negative feelings and result in an onset of stress, frustration, and exhaustion. At this point, if you learn to control your negativity and keep a more realistic outlook, you will remain motivated and try your best to fulfill the demands of your workplace. The internal satisfaction you receive from this will allow you to avoid all three early symptoms of burnout: stress, frustration, and exhaustion. It is common in the workplace for your boss to treat you unfairly. This may be due to personal dislike. Moreover, your job performance in the beginning was at a very high standard, and the boss may have felt that you might take his position in the future, so the boss created a difficult work environment for you.[20] This has happened in many places where I have worked, and it has happened to me. In response, I slowed down my performance level to gain my boss's confidence that I was not a threat and was not competing for the boss's position. I always seek to achieve a positive outcome and internal happiness, knowing that I can meet any kind of challenge to satisfy my mind and heart that I have worth and value in this world. In this way, you have a positive attitude and more

---

[18] Freudenberger, "Staff Burn-Out," 159; see also his book *Burnout: The High Cost of High Achievement* (New York: Anchor Press, 1980).

[19] Christina Maslach, "Burned-Out," *Human Behavior* 5, no. 9 (1976): 16–22.

[20] Douglas W. Bray, Richard J. Campbell, and Donald L. Grant, *Formative Years in Business: A Long-Term AT&T Study of Managerial Lives* (New York: Wiley, 1974).

self-confidence so that the people in the organization will start to come to you instead, and I will go to them. I never say no to additional projects at work. If a team is available to work on the project, then that is fine with me; otherwise, I will take full responsibility alone. I use my self-motivation, self-confidence, clear vision, clear goals, and know-how to implement a plan that generates a positive outcome by meeting the deadline, which comes from good time management skills. Remember the symptoms of early stress: overengagement, high emotions, hyperactivity followed by loss of energy, and anxiety, all of which may damage your health. Compare these feelings to the signs of early burnout: disengagement, blunted emotions, no new ideas, no motivation, and feelings of hopelessness, helplessness, isolation, and detachment that lead to depression and the belief that life is worthless, which can result in suicidal ideation and even a suicide attempt.

The root cause of burnout is embedded into your workplace. If you feel overworked and undervalued, then you are at higher risk of burnout.

Feeling frustrated and unappreciated leads to negative feelings and burnout among physicians and nurses. They are well-paid professionals, but in my opinion, they often have a lack of intrinsic motivation. This type of motivation leads to internal satisfaction and happiness and prevents burnout.

Frustration and exhaustion are a part of negative thinking and, combined with loss of interest in the workplace, can lead to burnout. Chronic stress leads to biochemical changes in the mind, which can cause depression. In extreme cases, this can lead to suicidal thoughts, and the victim may commit suicide because of feelings of worthlessness.

Primary care physicians should be willing to spend a little extra time to use the burnout screening tool found in chapter 4 in their clinical practice for any suspected workplace burnout in patients so that they can make an early diagnosis and prescribe treatment if required.

Conclusion

In my opinion, all physicians should know how to diagnose or screen for mental illness by having a good knowledge of the telltale signs and symptoms of anxiety and mood disorders. This knowledge will also be helpful for physicians themselves if they have early symptoms of burnout. If physicians have this self-awareness, then they can schedule an appointment with a psychologist or psychiatrist. People are hesitant to seek consultations because these visits will have future adverse effects on their jobs (i.e., mental health stigma). This may be a reason why people who are late to seek advice can damage their careers by becoming burned out or fired from their jobs. At this point, you must weigh what is important to you: carry the mental health stigma and ignore it, or identify and tackle it at its root to improve your quality of life. Burnout is being debated in the medical community as to how it should be defined.

Burnout has a very real effect on people's lives. We should not turn a blind eye to this. Burnout can involve a mental health stigma for employees, employers, and insurance providers. It is beneficial that a separate ICD-10 code (Z73.0: burnout as a state of vital exhaustion) now exists because it does not carry a mental health stigma. Primary care physicians, psychologists, and psychiatrists can provide effective treatment to severe burnout victims without jeopardizing their jobs or causing problems with insurance or worker's disability coverage. This is a complex issue. Therefore, we must focus more on the prevention aspects of burnout. The following are recommendations for both employees and employers to prevent burnout.

For Employees

+ Split your daily tasks into smaller pieces.
+ Consult with your supervisor to improve your performance.
+ Make your work environment friendly to overcome your deficiencies to performing well.
+ Consult an experienced coworker to guide you.
+ Try not to take your workplace issues home so that you can fully relax with your family.
+ Maintain a positive attitude and positive thinking in your life.
+ Negativity will always drain your energy and make you exhausted.
+ Consult the diagnostic criteria listed in the early or late onset of burnout questionnaires.

For Employers

+ Emotional rewards like kudos work well for daily minor jobs, but for bigger projects, external awards are helpful to convert expectations into reality.
+ Always try to motivate intrinsically when employees perform well. Teach them to accept challenges so that they gain more confidence after each positive outcome and feel internal happiness, which is key for these employees. They become energized to complete a task prior to the deadline and without suffering burnout symptoms.
+ Undertake training to identify early burnout in your employees and refer them for evaluation as per the workplace policy.

Medical Professionals

+ Try to make electronic health record (EHR) user friendly to improve process, simplicity in structuring, and easy-to-find outcome of search related to current lab and diagnostic tests result findings to save time of physician to avoid frustration and chronic stress. Usually EHR is overloaded with lot of unnecessary, time-wasting information that is not helpful to digesting lots of confusing information.

+ I think EHR designers need to further work with all stake-holders to make it simpler and save time for users so they can invest their time in patient care and not waste excess time in front of the screen. I think EHR should also internally collect attending physicians' accurate diagnostic and management plans as a separate icon in the EHR.

+ Our new generation is computer trained, and maybe they are not frustrated while trying to get patient information in EHR compared to more senior physicians. The latter may not be fast enough to accomplish finding or putting new information into the EHR because of the technology gap. These physicians have a higher risk of burnout than at any other phase of their careers.

+ I suggest bigger organizations hire medical scribes to help physicians to enter patient information into EHR according to physicians' note to save physicians' time and so they pay more attention to patient care. This will help prevent burnout among physicians and decrease suicide rates. If physicians are doing well, they can contribute salary for a scribe so that the mental health of our physicians can be improved and they can avoid overwhelming situation.

Awards and Honors

The following awards and award nominations were not my desire, but I received them due to the hospital administration's decision to nominate me for various awards in Saudi Arabia and the United States.

Nominated in 2016: Lifetime Achievement Award with the Association of Physicians of Pakistani Descent in North America (APPNA)

National Federal Recognition

The Chicago Federal Executive Board 2016, Finalist, Management Excellence Award.

Nominated: Jesse Brown Spirit Award, 2010–2016.

The Chicago Federal Executive Board Nominee for the 2015 Exceptional Professional Employee of the Year Award.

Received several special contribution, monitoring, and incentive awards between 2005 to 2019.

Nominated for the category of Outstanding Team Award in the Chicago metropolitan area for Chicago

Federal Employee of the Year in 2009, 2012, and 2013.

Nominated: Service to America Medal in 2006, 2007, and 2008. The Partnership and Atlantic Media Company—publisher of Government Executive, National Journal, and *The Atlantic*—created the Service to America Medals program in 2002 to publicly recognize outstanding federal employees who dedicate their lives to making a difference, which encourages a new generation to join the federal workforce. Nearly six hundred deserving public servants (out of ten million federal workforces) were nominated in the years 2006, 2007, and 2008. With so many compelling and inspiring stories, it was a real challenge to narrow the field to only thirty finalists.

Chicago Federal Employee of the Year 2006, Winner for the Program Specialist Category.

Recognition in the United States

Employee of the Year, 1997, Edgewater Medical Center, Chicago, Illinois, due to successfully and independently completing numerous projects and saving several thousands of dollars for the hospital.

International Recognition

1993—Certificate of Thanks and Recognition for Excellent Performance and Best Patient Care under Ministry of Health (MOH), Saudi Arabia

1992—Certificate for Enhancing Hospital Reputation through High Standards under MOH, Saudi Arabia

1990—Certificate for Excellent Job Performance and Best Patient Care under MOH, Saudi Arabia

1989—Best Hospital Employee under MOH, Saudi Arabia

References

Ahola, K., T. Honkonen, E. Isometsä, et al. "The Relationship between Job-related Burnout and Depressive Disorders—Results from the Finnish Health 20050 Study." *J Affect Dis* 88 (2005): 55–62 [PubMed].

Amoafo, E. N. Hanbali, A. Patel, and P. Singh. "What Are the Significant Factors Associated with Burnout in Doctors?" *Occup. Med.* 65 (2015): 117–121. DOI: 10.1093/occmed/kqu144 [PubMed].

Bakker, A., W. Schaufeli, M. Leiter, and T. Taris. "Work Engagement: An Emerging Concept in Occupational Health Psychology." *Work Stress* 3 (2008): 187–200. DOI: 1080/02678370802393649.

Breso, E., M. Salanova, and W. B. Schaufeli. "In Search of the Third Dimension of Burnout: Efficacy or Inefficacy?" *Applied Psychology* 56 (2007): 460–478.

"Diagnosing Burnout—Not as Easy as You Might Think." June 5, 2016. www.pauldechantmd.com/diagnosing-burnout.

Dyrbye, L. N., T. D. Shanafelt, C. M. Balch, D. Satele, J. Sloan, and J. Freischlag. "Relationship between Work-home Conflicts and Burnout among American Surgeons: A Comparison by

Sex." *Arch. Surg.* 146 (2011):211–217. DOI: 10.1001/arch-surg.2010.310 [PubMed].

Graham, J., H. W. W. Potts, and A. J. Ramirez. "Stress and Burnout in Doctors." *Lancet* 360 (2002): 1975–1976.

Hakanen, J., W. Schaufeli, and K. Ahola. "The Job Demands-Resources Model: A Three-year Cross-lagged Study of Burnout, Depression, Commitment, and Work Engagement." *Work Stress* 22 (2008): 224–241. DOI: 10.1080/02678370802379432.

Honkonen, T., K. Ahola, M. Pertovaara, et al. "The Association between Burnout and Physical Illness in the General Population—Results from the Finnish Health 2000 Study." *Journal of Psychosomatic Research* 61, no. 1 (2006): 59–66 [PubMed].

Joinson C. "Coping with Compassion Fatigue." *Nursing* 22, no. 4 (April 1992): 116,118–119, 120.

Leiter, M. P., and C. Maslach. "Areas of Work-life: A Structured Approach to Organizational Predictors of Job Burnout." In P. Perrewé & D. C. Ganster (eds.), *Research in Occupational Stress and Well-being* Vol. 3 (Oxford, UK: Elsevier, 2004), 91–134.

Leiter, M. P., and C. Maslach. *Preventing Burnout and Building Engagement: A Complete Program for Organizational Renewal.* San Francisco: Jossey Bass, 2000.

Lemaire, Jane B, and Jean E Wallace. "Burnout Among Doctors." *BMJ,* July 14, 2017. *https://doi.org/10.1136/bmj.j3360.*

Maslach C. and S. E. Jackson. "MBI: Human Services Survey for Medical Personnel." May 3, 2019, http://www.mindgarden.com/315-mbi-human-services-survey-medical-personnel.

Maslach, C., and M. P. Leiter. "Early Predictors of Job Burnout and Engagement." *Journal of Applied Psychology* 93 (2008): 498–512. DOI: 10.1037/0021-9010.93.3.498.

Maslach, Christina and Michael P. Leiter. "Understanding the Burnout Experience: Recent Research and Its Implications for Psychiatry." *World Psychiatry* 15, no. 2 (2016): 103–111.

Maslach, C., W. B. Schaufeli, and M. P. Leiter. "Job Burnout." *Annu Rev Psychol* 52 (2001): 397–422.

Osatuke, Katerine, Scott C. Moore, Christopher Ward, Sue R. Dyrenforth, and Linda Belton. "Civility, Respect, Engagement in the Workforce (CREW)." The Journal of Applied Behavioral Science 45, no. 3 (2009): 384–410. https://doi.org/10.1177/0021886309335067

Qualtrics. "7 Customer Expectations Types All Researchers Should Understand." June 25, 2018. Accessed July 14, 2018. https://www.qualtrics.com/blog/customer-expectations.

Shanafelt, T. D., O. Hasan, L. N. Dyrbye, C. Sinsky, D. Satele, J. Sloan, and C. P. West. "Changes in Burnout and Satisfaction with Work-life Balance in Physicians and the General US Working Population Between 2011 and 2014." *Mayo Clin. Proc.* 90 (2015): 1600–1613. DOI: 10.1016/j.mayocp.2015.08.023 [PubMed].

Taylor C., J. Graham, H. W. W. Potts, J. Candy, M. A. Richards, and A. J. Ramirez. "Impact of Hospital Consultants' Poor Mental

Health on Patient Care." *British Journal of Psychiatry* 190, no. 3 (2007): 268–269.

Taylor, C., J. Graham, H. W. W. Potts, M. A. Richards, and A. J. Ramirez. "Changes in Mental Health of UK Hospital Consultants since the Mid-1990s." The Lancet 366, no. 9487 (2005): 742–744. DOI: 10.1016/S0140-6736(05)67178-4.

"Workplace Stress." The American Institute of Stress, March 28, 2019. http://www.stress.org/workplace-stress.

Index

or antidepressant treatment by a referral to a psychiatrist 55
overstrain is used to indicate burnout xxix
overwhelmed xi, xiv, xix, xxxiv, 3, 4, 20, 25, 34, 53, 57, 60, 62, 65, 69, 77, 83, 89, 91, 101, 102, 105, 108, 114, 120, 130, 137, 138
Overwork 89

P

Parents' Role in Developing Childhood Personality to Prevent Future Burnout 124
Pathological (Negative) Stress 26
The Path to Pleasure and Happiness to Prevent Burnout 128
patients' xxi, xxix, 22, 32, 44, 53, 54, 60, 62, 69, 80, 134
personality plays an important role in developing future burnout 1
The Phases of the Burnout Process 86
Physical and Mental Fatigue 92
Physician Burnout 32, 33, 37, 38, 40, 41, 56, 58
physicians, xiii, xxi, 10, 32, 42, 44, 47, 69, 79, 149
police officers, xiii, xxi
poor work performance xxiv, 31
positive and hardworking mind-set 78
positive synchrony 13
Positive Thinking Leads to Intrinsic Motivation 128
potential victims xxv
power of self-management xxiv, xxix
Praise is an effective psychological tool 28
preventing burnout 36, 47, 136, 145, 158

Prevention of Future Burnout 122
primary care physician xv, xxiv, 51, 55, 56, 57, 58, 93, 94, 95, 96, 120, 148, 149
professionally talented human beings 24
prolonged stress xxv, 62, 82
proper guidelines to prepare medical students 39
psychiatric illness xiv, xxii, 34, 35, 85
psychoanalysis 24, 67
psychologist or psychiatrist xiv, xxiii, 48, 55, 86, 95, 96, 119, 149
psychosomatic illness, and hypochondriasis 27

Q

quick and easy understanding of the burnout process xxix

R

R&D department 74, 75
R&D with zero knowledge 75
ready to sacrifice your time, money, and sleep for your patients 39
Recognition in the United States 154
reduced autonomy, lack of enthusiasm and motivation, 62
Reduced personal accomplishment 11, 29
reduce social activity 61
The Relationship among Stress, Fear, and Negative Thinking 140
Relaxation xviii, xxxi, 46, 47, 55, 74, 92, 93, 101, 104, 106, 118, 125, 139, 146
relaxation techniques, 55, 101
residents, xiii, xxi, 10, 48, 79
resource imbalance 29

root cause of burnout is embedded into your workplace xxix, 64, 148

S

Saudi Arabia under the Ministry of Health (MOH) 71, 72, 77, 154, 155
Screening and Counseling 98
self-awareness xxiii, 8, 67, 129, 140, 145, 149
Self-Care Guide to the Early Phases of Burnout 108
self-confidence into an informed intuition. 2
Self-management of High Expectations 112
Sensing (S) xii, xiii, xiv, xxi, xxiv, xxvi, xxxi, 4, 5, 6, 7, 12, 13, 17, 18, 20, 21, 22, 24, 27, 28, 37, 40, 43, 44, 45, 49, 52, 55, 65, 66, 67, 68, 69, 74, 76, 79, 81, 82, 84, 87, 91, 98, 99, 103, 104, 108, 112, 116, 118, 121, 127, 129, 131, 132, 133, 134, 136, 142, 145, 147, 149, 153, 159
a series of interconnected events of signs and symptoms 86
seven customer expectations 20
show flexibility or quick adaptability to overcome stress 47
Simple Stress (Feelings of Pressure or Tension) 12, 102, 103, 104, 108
simplify the mechanisms of burnout 12
Situational Expectations 23
situational stresses xvii, 23, 54, 145
social relationships 2
social workers, xiii, xxi, 10, 31

Static Performance Expectations 21
Step-by-Step Self-Care Solution of Burnout 98
Stress Control 116, 140
Stress Management Prevents Burnout in General Workplace Population and Health-care Professionals 140
stress reaction 26, 140
Successful expectations 17
suppression of emotion xxvii
Surround Yourself with Positive Thinkers 132
survival strategies 35

T

teachers, xiii, xxi, 10, 11, 31
Teaching Stress-Control Management and Internal Happiness 137
teaming with a mentor to improve work performance 55
team works hard to shape this expectation into reality 17
Technological Expectations 22
thinking styles, xxvii, 12
Thinking (T) xi, xvii, xxvii, xxxi, xxxiii, 1, 2, 4, 5, 6, 7, 9, 12, 14, 15, 18, 25, 26, 27, 28, 32, 33, 34, 35, 36, 40, 42, 44, 46, 47, 55, 61, 65, 66, 67, 69, 70, 71, 72, 75, 81, 84, 89, 90, 91, 98, 100, 101, 103, 104, 111, 113, 116, 117, 119, 120, 122, 123, 126, 127, 128, 129, 130, 131, 132, 133, 134, 136, 140, 141, 142, 143, 146, 147, 148, 150, 157, 158, 159
Time Management Prevents Stress 138